MW00992866

INHERITANCE
Your Best Life Later

How God uses your time, talent, and treasure to
advance the gospel and increase your joy

David Choe
Edited by Michelle Choe

Contents

Introduction

A few years ago my pastor shared with the elders how he personalized a Bible for each of his kids. He spent one year and wrote in the margins his thoughts as he highlighted certain passages. "So, when I die, they'll have something to remember from me," he said. I thought that was a grand idea and decided to embark upon a similar journey. At the time, Michelle and I had four children, so my plan was to spend the next four years journaling in the margins of their Bibles.

At the same time I had just entered a career transition into asset management, where as an investment professional, my colleagues and I would create stock portfolios for our clients. As part of this career transition, I started studying to earn the Chartered Financial Analyst® credential[1]. Anyone familiar with these exams can attest that they completely consume your life until you pass all three exams. The failure rate for each of the exams is very high, so there was a strong possibility I would have to take the exams multiple times.

Studying hundreds of hours for the exams and studying the Bible for hundreds of hours at the same time caused me to start seeing things. No, I wasn't hallucinating, but I started noticing verses about finance and economics all over the Bible.

> *Whoever is **generous** to the poor **lends** to the LORD, and he will **repay** him for his deed. Proverbs 19:17*
>
> *Therefore if you have not been faithful in the **unrighteous mammon**, who will commit to **your trust** the **true riches**? Luke 16:11*
>
> *But remember the LORD your God, for it is he who gives you the ability to **produce wealth**. Deuteronomy 8:18*
>
> *And whatever you do, do it heartily, as to the Lord and not to men, knowing that from the Lord you will receive the **reward of the inheritance**; for you serve the Lord Christ. Colossians 3:23 – 24*

Everywhere in my daughter's Bible I was highlighting in neon green the verses about incentives, rewards, money, inheritance, treasure, wealth, etc.

---

[1] The CFA Institute owns the CFA designation for Chartered Financial Analyst®.

These were not dozens of verses; they were hundreds of verses. But one particular narrative caught my eye.

> *If you love those who love you, what* **credit** *is that to you? Even sinners love those who love them. And if you do good to those who are good to you, what* **credit** *is that to you? Even sinners do that... But love your enemies, do good to them, and lend to them without expecting to get anything back.* **Then your reward will be great,** *and you will be children of the Most High, because he is kind to the ungrateful and wicked. Luke 6:32 – 33, 35 NIV*

Why didn't Jesus say, "If you love those who love you--that is not right!" Why didn't he use more idealistic language? Why should we care if the love we give has any "charis[2]," or grace-credit for ourselves? And why does Jesus then promise a reward for doing good? I've read this passage dozens of times in the past, but this time, it jumped out at me.

Then one cold and blistery morning on Feb 21, 2014, I drove about four hours to a men's prayer retreat. Because of the blizzard-like conditions, I started at 4 A.M. and drove about 20 MPH. While I drove, I experienced a wonderful quiet time of meditation and reflection. I asked myself this question: "What endures for eternity? Why do finance professionals value businesses according to the perpetuity value (the portion of the business that hypothetically goes on forever)?" And then it hit me. All value comes from a basis of eternal value and is adjusted accordingly. For example, the minute participants in the stock market believe a company is in danger of going bankrupt, its valuation plummets to its "fire sale" value. The valuation goes from being based on perpetuity to its "scrap" value. Valuations are based on what endures for eternity. The Bible tells us what endures unto eternity; it is **the glory of God.**

So, after the retreat I went home and categorized all of the verses about what endures forever as assets, what is temporary as liabilities, and what remains as inheritance or equity.

What the verses revealed are the following: Through justification, we are saved. We pass from death to life and enter a new reality. What is that reality? God puts us on this earth and invests in us TIME, TALENT, and TREASURE. These things are temporary. Our job is to take these temporary gifts that God invests in us and convert them into what is

---

[2] The word "charis" is the Greek word for "grace." The reason that for this passage that translators have translated it as "credit" is because of the cause-effect relationship between obedience and reward.

eternal: the Word (in our heart), godliness, spiritual children, the Church, and the kingdom. All of these are what the Bible refers to as "fruit." The fruit we produce (assets) based on the resources God gives us (liabilities) determines our heavenly treasure (equity). Converting time, talent, and treasure into eternal assets is how the kingdom advances so that the Great Commission might be fulfilled. God promises extravagant rewards for joining his mighty work of redemption!

This book is about paradigm shifts. In order to find joy in our purpose on this earth, we must change how we think about our lives. As we go through scripture together here are a few insights to look for:

- In man's economy time, talent, and earthly treasure are assets. In God's economy they are a loan.
- Having a lot of resources is not bad. To not use them for the glory of God is a terrible sin that will be judged.
- We don't all get the same reward. We can make our heavenly treasure as big as we want it to be.
- It's not wrong to be motivated by heavenly reward. In fact, when we want treasure later, we will be godly now.

This life is a dress rehearsal for the real life, the life that is to come. The life that is to come is the real thing. It will go on forever. What will our assignment be in the next life for the glory of God? It will largely depend on what we do with this life. If we actually believed that were true, then we would see an explosion of grace-filled energy to be godly disciples and to spread the gospel to the ends of the earth. Though this life is full of suffering, we press on for the joy set before us. Our inheritance awaits us.

I pray as we dive through scripture together, the eyes of your heart will be enlightened so that you will know the riches of his glorious inheritance in the saints (Ephesians 1:19). By the end of this book, it is my prayer that the Holy Spirit will convict your heart, give you passion for the gospel, and give you a vision of how to use your time, talent, and treasure for the glory of God.

Part 1

The Glory of God and God's Economy

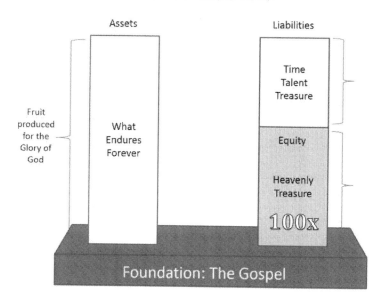

Eternal Balance Sheet

Chapter 1 – God's Economy
The Weight of Glory

I am the LORD; that is my name; my glory I give to no other, nor my praise to carved idols. Isaiah 42:8

There is a weight[3] to the glory of God. His glory is not something we treat lightly. God's highest concern is upholding the glory of his name (Isaiah 48:11). His name encapsulates his character, his nature, and his distinctiveness. The weightiness of the glory of God is so heavy, that God does not tolerate even the slightest transgression of his holiness.[4] Is this because God is, as certain atheists try to argue, cantankerous and easily offended? No. The plumb line of the universe is upheld by this perfect standard of his holiness and glory. Up is up and down is down because all definitions come from the unshakeable foundation of God himself. The very laws of physics flow from his character and nature (Romans 1:20). Hence, the universe could not exist without God upholding an objective standard, based on the highest standard, the glory of his own name. The entire universe is held together by the word of Christ, who is the very radiance of the glory of God (Hebrews 1:3). As we study scripture and contemplate the depth of the riches of the glory of God, we see that his glory is the highest good (Romans 11:33-36).

When God created the material universe, he flung into existence millions of myriad creatures, objects, and phenomenon with varied shapes, colors, and sizes to show his eternal nature and divine power (Romans 1:20). And when God looked at creation, he said it was "very good" (Genesis 1:31). The creation revealed beauty, complexity, symmetry, simplicity, awesomeness, and majesty that hinted at the glory of the unseen God. And God created man as the apex of his glory to rule the seen world in a manner in which the eternal Father rules the unseen world.[5] His intent was that all of creation would erupt in praise and worship of the Creator, beholding the glory and splendor of God's majesty in that which was created (Psalm 19:1-5).

---

[3] The word for glory in Hebrew is "chabod," which comes from the root word "chabad," which means "heavy." His glory is heavy in the way a storehouse of treasure is heavy laden with riches. It's overflowing with abundance.

[4] Observant Jews don't even utter the word YHWH because they hold such a high view of his name.

[5] Genesis 1:26 speaks of God making man in "our image" (Trinitarian view). "Let them have dominion over the fish of the sea...birds...cattle..." In Psalm 8:2-8, the author recounts how man was created to have dominion over the work of God's hands. Hebrews 2:5-8 reiterates the purpose in creating mankind. Christ fulfilled the promise and we await our joining this fulfillment.

But Adam and Eve doubted God's word when they listened to Satan. *Did God really say* (Genesis 3:1)? Adam and Eve doubted both God's promises and God's warnings. Adam usurped the role of God as arbiter over good and evil when he ate of the Tree of Knowledge of Good and Evil. This usurping of what belongs to God alone is the essence of sin. Sin is *hamartia*[6], falling short of the glory of God (Romans 3:23). To sin is to miss the mark of what God intended man to do. Man was supposed to reflect God's glory (2 Corinthians 3:18). Instead man decided to exalt himself and steal God's glory. We see this very clearly in Genesis 11, at the Tower of Babel.

> *Come, let us build ourselves a city, and a tower whose top is in the heavens; let us **make a name for ourselves**... Genesis 11:4*

The height of arrogance is to make a name for yourself when God has already named you. God named and created Adam as his image bearer (Genesis 1:27.) Adam named the creatures (Genesis 2:19). But after the Fall, Adam heard God's call and hid. Human history is this: man rejects God's call to bear witness to his glory and seeks to make a name for himself. From kingdoms rising to kingdoms falling, man has continually sought to exalt his own glory. We see this arrogance exemplified when King Nebuchadnezzar of Babylon declared,

> *Is not this great Babylon, that I have built for a royal dwelling by my mighty power and for the honor of my majesty? Daniel 4:30*

Preferring glory apart from the glory of God stirs up the wrath of God. God is not angry that we do "bad things," per se[7], but that we constantly prefer what is light and flimsy to the weightiness of God's glory. We prefer the creature over the Creator (Romans 1:21-22). We prefer our own image over the image of his Son. We prefer earthly pleasure above heavenly treasure. We are in essence, telling God that his glory has no weight. We are telling God that his glory is flimsy and our glory is weighty (Isaiah 5:20, Proverbs 3:7). And so we have stored up wrath against ourselves (Romans 2:5).

---

[6] The Hebrew word for sin is *hamartia,* which means "missing the mark."

[7] God of course hates all sin. My point is that some evangelicals use driving over the speed limit, telling a white lie, or stealing a pen from work to make the point that we are all convicted sinners. Many unbelievers thus view sin as simply having a few "human flaws" and that God is thin-skinned and easily offended at our shortcomings. Rather, we are bold-faced rebels and usurpers who flaunt our defiance of God's laws by constantly viewing our ways as the right way. We believe we are the exception to the rule as long as we don't commit murder or rape.

If God did not care about the weightiness of his own glory, he could simply brush aside the transgression and say, "I'm not offended!" But if God were to do that, then God would be lying. God would be declaring that his glory has no weight. No, the offense is stealing God's glory. This stealing incurs a debt. The debt is so great, that no amount of offering or sacrifice could repay that debt apart from blood (Hebrews 9:22). Think of the weight of God's glory like an infinite stack of gold bars, and each bar of infinite weight. Stealing from the treasury of God's glory must be paid with something of equal value. Simply saying "sorry" is not good enough. And nothing in all creation has comparable weight in glory.

God had to pay for this stealing of glory with something of commensurate value, the blood of his own Son. By paying for our sins with the death of his own Son, God the Father declared his own worth, thus upholding the integrity of his own glory (Romans 3:25-26). This is why no one is justified by works (Romans 3:20). Can we put forth our "good deeds" and declare to God that the weight of our goodness equals the weight of the glory we've stolen? Utter foolishness! Our righteousness apart from Christ is like filthy rags (Isaiah 64:6), whitewashed tombs, and dead men's bones (Matthew 23:27). Rather than impress God, our works of righteousness only bring condemnation and wrath (Galatians 3:10, Romans 4:15). Do any of us really want to stand before God Almighty seeking to justify ourselves?

The most humble thing a man can do is to bend his knees before Almighty God and call himself what he truly is, a sinner (Luke 18:13). And instead of exalting our own deeds, our own track record, we simply call on the name of the Lord (Romans 10:13). This belief in our helpless state and in Christ's sufficiency is faith. And that faith saves us (Ephesians 2:8-9). And just like creatures know their master, faith acknowledges we are no longer the masters of our own destiny and calls Christ as "Lord" (Isaiah 1:3, 1 Corinthians 12:3). God names us heirs and declares us "justified!"

When we experience a *metanoia*[8], a repentance, a changing of the mind, Jesus goes from being a part of my life to being everything in my life. Jesus goes from being somewhat important to being all important. Advancing God's name goes from being part of my bucket list to being the only item on the bucket list. *"He must increase, and I must decrease" (John 3:30).*

---

[8] The Greek word for repentance is "metanoia." It means to change one's mind. Most preachers jump ahead to the result of metanoia, which is to change one's direction. Commonly, many pastors will liken repentance to walking in one direction and then walking in the opposite direction. This is a correct consequence but skips the vital change in one's thinking, namely valuing Christ correctly.

Acknowledging God's lordship creates a deposit into our inheritance (Ephesians 1:4). The Holy Spirit seals it and fills our hearts with confidence (2 Corinthians 1:22). We hand over to God the title-deed to our lives, with full faith and confidence (Philippians 1:6). Since we were bought with a price, his redemption makes us bond-servants (1 Corinthians 6:20). This bond is not a sin-debt-note that we must pay off to earn justification. No, only Christ's perfection both satisfies God's wrath and puts us in right standing. Instead, think of this bond like a promissory note in which we voluntarily indenture ourselves to spreading God's love (Romans 13:8). In return, God recompenses everything we do for his glory and multiplies it one-hundred fold (Mark 10:30) into our inheritance account (Revelation 22:12).

God gives us three liability accounts in this life: time, talent, and treasure (Ephesians 5:16, Matthew 25:15, Luke 16:11, Luke 12:48).[9] Time, talent, and treasure are liabilities, a loan if you will, because we owe God our very lives (Matthew 6:24). They are resources he has invested into our stewardship. Our resources are temporal and are fading away (2 Corinthians 4:18). He deposits into those liability accounts grace-gifts, or *dynamos*[10] (Matthew 25:15). God is looking to see if his bond-servants value the weight of his glory. Will we multiply these temporal gifts and then convert them into eternal assets (Matthew 25:20-21, Luke 16:9-12)? God's temporal gifts of time, talent, and treasure create a test: Do we value what is eternal?

If what is most valuable to God is the glory of his own name, then valuing God's glory means taking those gifts of time, talent, and treasure and applying it toward this vision:

> *that at the name of Jesus every knee should bow, of those in heaven, and of those on earth, and of those under the earth, and that every tongue should confess that Jesus Christ is Lord, to the glory of God the Father. Philippians 2:10-11*

Are we motivated toward that vision? The system that God puts in place to orchestrate, monitor, supervise, and account for all of these grace gifts deployed for the exaltation of Christ is called a *dispensation*. Dispensation means "stewardship," or the wise use of resources that God has delegated to us. What God has given his bond-servants are time, talent, and treasure for

---

[9] A liability account is a loan. It is an investment in which you are required or obligated to produce something of greater value with.

[10] "Dynamos" literally means "power" in Greek. In the Parable of the Talents, Jesus says he gives the money according to each person's skill, or "dynamos." That is why we both our natural abilities and our spiritual gifts are "grace gifts."

the purpose of advancing his kingdom. The Greek word for dispensation is "oikonomia," or "economy."

> *If indeed you have heard of the **dispensation**[11] of the grace of God which was given to me for you, how that by revelation He made known to me the mystery... which in other ages was not made known to the sons of men, as it has now been revealed by the Spirit to his holy apostles and prophets: that the **Gentiles** should be fellow **heirs**, of the same body, and **partakers**[12] **of his promise** in Christ through the gospel. Ephesians 3:2-6*

God promised to Abraham that all the nations would be blessed through his seed (Genesis 22:18). How can the birthright be transferred to those outside of Israel? The answer is the gospel. Paul reveals this mystery: the Gentiles are partakers (Greek: *koinonos* – sharers, shareholders) of the same inheritance (*kléronomeó*[13] – allotment, shares) as the Jews when they receive Christ by faith. The inheritance is something greater than anything we can have in this life. It is incorruptible, undefiled, does not fade, and is reserved in heaven for God's people (1 Peter 1:4).

This is exciting. God's Spirit is in the process of gathering the nations to culminate at the judgment seat of Christ where every knee will bow and every tongue will confess that "Jesus Christ is Lord." You and I, by grace alone through faith alone in Christ alone, are now invited into this mighty work of God (Ephesians 4:12). The works of the law are abolished (Ephesians 2:15) and we are invited into this new kingdom reality where our grace-works (Ephesians 2:10) advance the kingdom forward until the earth is filled with the knowledge of God like the waters cover the sea (Habakkuk 2:14). I want to be a part of that, don't you?

God's economy is designed so that the Church will stop hoarding the blessings of God and will press on in the Spirit to advance the gospel of the glory of God. And the crazy thing is, God promises a reward for all of this. Not only do we get to participate in something so cosmically important, we get to find purpose, meaning, and joy in God's unfolding plan (Romans 8:28). It's like sitting on the sidelines of the Super Bowl and then the coach points to you in the stands, makes you suit up, gives you a pep talk, and then let's you play. What?!? Oh, and then you score the next touchdown. We shouldn't be allowed to go anywhere near the ball, but the coach says, "You

---

[11] Greek: "Oikonomia" or Economy, which refers to the management or stewardship of God's kingdom
[12] Greek: "Koinonos" or Sharers, those who share in the inheritance of the kingdom
[13] Greek: "Kleronomeo" or Allotment; With the two Words for "sharers" and "allotment" I connect the modern day terms "shareholders" and "shares" to the financial term "equity."

are key to this play." As difficult as it is to fathom, it's true; in the midst of God's sovereignty, he chooses to use faulty, fallible vessels to finish his work on earth (2 Corinthians 4:7).

My heart wonders if we're in the ninth inning of human history. Will the Church in America wake up to its awesome privilege and responsibility or will we fade into post-Christian darkness? Will we remember our first love, or will our lampstand be removed?[14] I'm hoping and praying that simply teaching what scripture has to say about your inheritance will motivate you. I am hoping and praying that the Spirit will excite within you a desire to go all out for the gospel and the glory of God. And I'm hoping that your love of God will enhance, not diminish your desire for heavenly treasure. Our inheritance awaits us.

---

[14] The notion of likening the church's vitality to a lampstand comes from Revelation 2:5. Jesus accuses the Church in Philadelphia of losing its first love. He admonishes them to repent lest he remove their lampstand. Apparently they did not heed the warning. If you travel to the site of the Philadelphian Church in modern day Turkey, you will only find ruins.

Chapter 2 – The Eternal Balance Sheet

*Each one's work will become clear; for the Day will declare it, because it will be revealed by fire; and the fire will test each one's work, of what sort it is. If anyone's work which he has built on it **endures,** he will receive a **reward.** If anyone's work is **burned,** he will suffer **loss;** but he himself will be saved, yet so as through fire.   1 Corinthians 3:13-15*

God is a perfect judge, a perfect evaluator. Unlike us, he sees the heart and he sees our intentions and motivations. All of this, hidden and in plain view will be judged one day and God will reward us for that which remains after the fire of his testing occurs. What I'd like to propose is a visualization tool that will help you understand how you're building up kingdom assets in this lifetime that will result in greater and greater treasure.

In finance, there is a simple tool called the balance sheet. Essentially, you have three types of accounts: assets, liabilities, and equity. Assets are those items that produce income. Liabilities are those items for which you incur a debt. Equity, or wealth, is whatever remains. **Assets minus liabilities equal equity**. We understand this very simply from our home mortgage. If you buy a $200k house with a $200k mortgage and the value of the home (asset) appreciates the next year to $300k, then $300k minus $200k equal your net wealth, your equity of $100k. That's a nice profit. Contrariwise, if the house you bought for $200k depreciates to an asset value of $150k, then $150k assets minus $200k liabilities equal -$50k loss to your wealth or equity.

In the same way, God is saying our life work is like building a house (asset) and God our judge will evaluate our life work at the end of this age. He's going to look at our asset value (kingdom impact, harvest, godliness) and subtract all the uninvested resources he assigned us in this life as a liability (talent, money, education, influence, resources). Our kingdom equity is based on what we produce relative to what we've been given. In understanding the resources God has given us (liabilities), the outcomes he is expecting from us (assets), hopefully we will be motivated to grow the treasure that he will reward us (equity).

Assets minus Liabilities = Equity

Eternal Balance Sheet

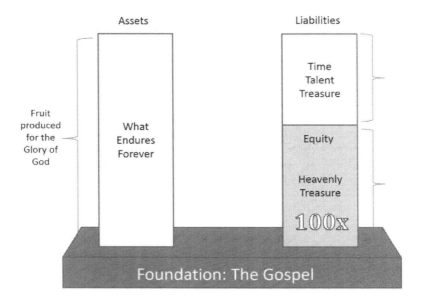

Assets - For the earth will be filled with the knowledge of the glory of the Lord, as the waters cover the sea. Habakkuk 2:14

God deposits in us temporal resources (liabilities)[15] to produce eternal fruit (assets). When I began to contemplate what the Lord expects as fruit, I asked myself, "What does the Bible say endures forever?" Here's what I found:

> *The Word of God - The grass withers, the flower fades, but the **Word** of our God stands **forever**. Isaiah 40:8*

> *Godliness - For bodily exercise profits a little, but godliness is **profitable** for all things, having promise of the life that **now** is and of that which is **to come**. 1 Timothy 4:8*

---

[15] Liabilities are like debt financing. Here's how debt investment works. You invest debt and produce a profit at a higher rate of return than the cost of borrowing. With the excess profits you pay down the debt and literally multiply your equity. In finance, this is called "leverage." It works in the opposite direction as well. God invests time, talent, and treasure into our lives so that we produce a leveraged return for his glory.

*Offspring and Spiritual Offspring –The **fruit** of the righteous is a tree of life; and he who wins souls is wise. Proverbs 11:30*

*The Church –And I say also unto thee, that thou art Peter, and upon this rock I will build my church; and the **gates of hell shall not prevail** against it. Matthew 16:18*

*The Kingdom of God – But **seek ye first** the kingdom of God, and his righteousness; and **all these things shall be added** unto you. Matthew 6:33*

*Legacy – Not that I seek **the gift**, but I seek the **fruit** that abounds to your **account**. Philippians 4:17*

Assets are the fruit of your labors. By God's grace, the Holy Spirit implants the Word of God in you. You meditate on it and your thoughts are transformed. Because you experience a *metanoia*, a change of mind, your desires start to change. You begin to hate sin and love God's righteousness. This produces the fruit of godliness. Growing in the Word and growing in godliness is the essence of being a disciple, an imitator of Christ. Then you multiply that seed and produce the fruit of righteousness in others as you share the Word and win souls to Christ. They become disciples in the Church and grow to full spiritual maturity. We, the Church, then take the vision of the Great Commission, and bring the gospel and total life transformation all over the world.

The final asset account is your legacy. Your legacy is the fruit that **others** produce that is credited to **your** account. Paul tells the Philippian Church that their gifts supporting his ministry would be credited to their account. Think about this. Paul's faithful, fruitful service for the Lord gets credited to the Philippian Church's eternal balance sheet. Imagine getting some of Billy Graham's fruit credited to your account. This thought should REALLY motivate us toward spiritual multiplication if we indeed take growing our heavenly treasure seriously. Do you want your heavenly equity to be huge? Multiply your assets by investing in other fruit producing, faithful believers.

Liabilities—For everyone to whom much is given, from him much will be required. Luke 12:48b

Why do we say, "Don't squander what God has given you?" or, "Don't waste your life on that which doesn't last?" What we are saying is an agreement with the scripture, *"For everyone to whom much is given, from him much will be required."* We have this notion in our minds that there is a reason why

God gives us talents, abilities, knowledge, resources. Even unbelievers know this is true. God has implanted the idea that we were meant for something more. We were meant to take all that God has entrusted with us in this life and make something beautiful out of it. The lifelong conundrum we face is this twofold dilemma of, "What's my purpose?" and "Who will get the glory?" How we use our productive capacity answers the first question. Our entire life record of whether we lived for God's glory or our own glory will reveal whether we are a sheep or a goat.

Back to liabilities, we know that what we are given in this life is a liability, not the kind of liability that is like a debilitating condition. It's a liability in the sense that it is **borrowed** resources like a **loan**. They don't belong to you. Even non-Christians resonate with this concept. You will often hear non-Christians who have attained some measure of success say, "I feel like I need to give back" or "I'm living on **borrowed time**" or "My **talent is on loan** from God."

What are these temporary resources that God has entrusted in me?

> *TIME – Redeeming the time, because the days are evil. Galatians 5:15*
>
> *TALENT - Train up a child in the way he should go, and when he is old he will not depart from it. Proverbs 22:6*
>
> *TREASURE – For where your treasure is, there your heart will be also. Matthew 6:21*

Over the course of your life (TIME), you go through a process to grow your potential (TALENT), with the goal of creating wealth that you can eventually transfer (TREASURE).

What may shock you is that the earthly treasure [i.e. money] you've accumulated in this life is a liability. Wealth is an asset in man's economy but it is a liability in God's economy. The more you accumulate, the more God expects you to produce kingdom assets with. Remember, assets minus liabilities equal equity. Kingdom impact relative to all the resources you've been entrusted with determine your heavenly reward. All that cash you have accumulating and have not earmarked for the kingdom will be held against you like that talent that was buried. God expects us to deploy everything we have on our balance sheet to advance his kingdom and his glory.

Liability = Opportunity. God gives us temporary resources to advance his eternal kingdom. We are in the beginning stages of the LARGEST intergenerational wealth transfer in the history of the world. We are talking TENS of TRILLIONS of dollars that will pass from generation to generation.

And if we were only talking about evangelicals, that would still equate to TRILLIONS[16]. Many, if not most retired evangelicals have not thought about how all of those resources will pass to the next generation in a way that maximizes kingdom impact and the advancement of the gospel. God will call all of that into account. Our heavenly reward is at stake.

Equity - that you may know what is the hope of his calling, what are the riches of the glory of his inheritance in the saints. Ephesians 1:18b

Your heavenly treasure looks a lot like equity. Equity is the remainder of all the assets produced relative to the amount of liabilities it required to produce profit. Equity is the return on the investment. Equity is the profit. Equity is the gain. Every time you read in scripture about profit, gain, or reward think "equity value."

Equity is a powerful concept that impacts all of your life. If you bought 1,000 shares of Apple stock at $7 (during CEO Steve Jobs' tenure) and held it to his passing, you would have realized a 100x return. Here's what's great about equity. As it grows, your joy increases! Monitor your own feelings as you watch the stock price of a company you own go up. Or think how happy you feel when you know your home value is appreciating. God gives us joy now based on equity you will receive later.

Jesus admonishes us to "store up treasures for ourselves in heaven." He's literally urging us to hoard it on the other side. And rather than result in selfishness, storing up treasure in heaven will result in humility, service, generosity, and love. In order to be great you and I must become the servant of all (Matthew 23:11).

As I contemplated this concept of equity and Jesus' admonishment this thought dawned on me: **We can make our eternal equity as big as we want it to be**! That concept may sound crazy but as you read the scriptures

---

[16] As of Mar 6, 2014, U.S. household net wealth reached $80.7 Trillion.
http://online.wsj.com/news/articles/SB10001424052702303824204579423183397213204
In Wikipedia, the top 1% of earners account for approximately 35% of this wealth. Assuming none of them are Christians (not true, but for the sake of argument), we are left with $52.5T. If evangelicals account for 25% of the U.S. population, then evangelicals control approximately $13 Trillion of wealth, which is the size of the entire GDP of China in purchasing power parity. (source: Wikipedia)

I will highlight, you will see that running the race of life [to win], will produce heaping treasure.

Assets minus Liabilities equal Equity

God takes the equity of our fruitfulness and he multiplies it 100x (Mark 10:30). We are faithful with a little and God rewards us with much. God's use of equity demonstrates both his fairness and his generosity. Sometimes we think that receiving God's grace means, "Nothing counts toward reward, because we all get the same thing." We have confused justification with assignment. We are justified by Christ's righteousness alone. Nothing we can do can add to that perfection. Equity in our heavenly treasure is about our role in the life to come. And because God is perfectly fair as well as generous, when we think about equity we should think, "Everything counts." That is why Jesus said that our heavenly Father will judge even every careless word we utter (Matthew 12:36). Why? Because words are fruit and fruit accrues toward our heavenly treasure. In God's economy we are living in the dispensation of grace, the kind of grace that empowers us to live for the glory of God. And in this dispensation, everything counts toward our eternal equity.

The Equity Mindset

Wanting and eagerly desiring heavenly treasure will create a massive paradigm shift in how we live now. Today pessimism pervades evangelical culture. We often exhibit a "circle the wagons" mentality. An over-obsession with End Times theology has resulted not in an extraordinary push for the gospel, but in the Church retreating into its sub-culture, untouched by the world.

As an equity analyst, one of the most evident indicators I observe in great management teams is that they know their core business and continuously reinvest profits to grow, regardless of economic conditions. They invest when everyone else is running for the hills. Their competitors retrench in the middle of external difficulty. Great management teams double down and accelerate their market share gains. Recessions are often the best opportunities for explosive growth.

If we are indeed living in the End-Times, now is not the time to circle the wagons. Now is the time to double down on the gospel and finish the Great Commission until that work is complete or Christ returns. Our heavenly treasure is at stake.

Eternal Balance Sheet

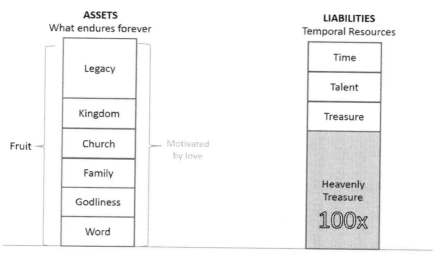

Chapter 3 – Foundations of God's Economy
Why does God use incentives?

Looking for that blessed hope, and the glorious appearing of our great God, and our savior, Jesus Christ. Titus 2:13

When was the last time you heard a sermon about heaven? When was the last time you thought about heaven? What do you think it will be like? Why is it that when we think about heaven we think in terms of the colors white, gold, and blue? Why do our minds drift to sitting in clouds, floating around, strumming harps, and doing nothing but singing hymns? Our inaccurate, unbiblical thoughts about heaven create precisely the lack of motivation for living godly lives on earth. To be all we can be for King Jesus, we've got to think clearly about our reward in heaven and our life afterward.

For example, why do some people believe we are going to be floating around in the clouds?

> *For the creation was subjected to futility, not willingly, but because of Him who subjected it in hope; because the* **creation itself also will be delivered from the bondage of corruption** *into the glorious liberty of the children of God. For we know that the whole creation groans and labors with birth pangs together until now. Not only that, but we also who have the first fruits of the Spirit, even we ourselves groan within ourselves, eagerly waiting for the adoption, the* **redemption** *of our* **body.** *Romans 8:20-23*

Do you read that? At the resurrection we are not going to be disembodied spirits floating around. Our bodies will be real! The remade creation will be real! Sin started a principle of decay and death in this present world. And as glorious as we think nature is, it is a pale shadow of what it will be. So much so, that all of creation is waiting for the day to burst out of the cocoon of death to a new glorious state. If you think the colors of New England in the fall are brilliant, just wait for the new earth! If you watched the series "Planet Earth" in high definition with awe and wonder, just wait for the new earth! If you think that a house with an ocean view is spectacular, just wait and see what your mansion in glory will look like!

Do you yearn for this? Or is it completely uninspiring to you? This is your birthright. What we have here in this life is nice, it serves a function, but it is a bowl of Esau's soup[17] in comparison with the inheritance waiting for us.

This is what drives me to distraction with the so-called prosperity gospel. Purveyors of prosperity theology elevate all the blessings of our inheritance and magnify receiving them NOW, in their corruptible form. No! Our inheritance is incorruptible, undefiled, reserved in heaven (1 Peter 1:4). So, while there may be nothing wrong with having or receiving lots of material blessings on this earth, to set your affections upon them distracts us from our purpose on this earth, which is to advance the kingdom. This life is one big test of *delayed gratification*. We are to set our affections, our deepest desires on heaven, not on what God can give us today (Colossians 3:20). When we go into "name it, claim it" mode, we are acting like the Prodigal Son who told his father that he wanted his inheritance immediately. He devalued his inheritance.

To value our inheritance properly, it's useful to think about what we are hoping for. As much as in this life you may feel squeamish about "hope," and getting your hopes up, and getting your hopes crushed, I urge you to hope in Christ. Look forward to the hope of his coming (Titus 2:13) and the reward he will bring with him (Revelation 22:12). Get your hopes up! Ratchet your hopes higher. When the Bible uses terms like "more than we could ask or imagine" (Ephesians 3:20), that is an encouragement to imagine.

So what are we getting?

> The Church will reign with Jesus over the whole universe. Ephesians 1:21
> We get bodies that will be perfect. Romans 8:23
> Our bodies will be glorified and radiant. Matthew 13:43
> We will live in mansions of glory. John 14:2
> We will have purpose and meaning in work. Matthew 25:23
> We will receive recognition in the presence of the saints and angels from God himself. Matthew 25:23
> We will have responsibility exponentially applied to our stewardship. Matthew 25:23
> We will receive reward on top of that stewardship. Matthew 25:28

---

[17] In Genesis 25:27-34 the Bible tells of two brothers Jacob and Esau. Esau was the firstborn of Isaac and heir to the family inheritance. One day, Esau came back from hunting completely famished. Because he lacked self-control, he asked Jacob to feed him some lentil soup. In exchange, Esau promised to give Jacob his birthright. The Bible says, "Esau despised his birthright." (v. 37) That is where the "bowl of soup" allusion comes from.

We will eat and feast at the wedding supper. Matthew 25:10
We will receive 100-fold houses and lands according to our
sacrifice. Mark 10:30
We will have authority over angels. 1 Corinthians 6:3
We who persevere under trial will receive a crown. James 1:12

What's astounding in reading about what is waiting for us in the next life is that it is über[18], über, über lavish and extravagant, almost embarrassingly so. And rather than reading, "Oh be modest! Modesty is a virtue," the Bible portrays our heavenly reward as over the top.

And here's the crazy thing about thinking about heaven: it leads to ALL the right behaviors today.

We will live soberly, righteously and godly in this present world.
Titus 2:12
We will be the servant of all. Mark 9:35
We will be generous. Luke 6:38
We will give in a way that won't puff ourselves up. Matthew 6:4
We will pray in a way to not make ourselves look good.
Matthew 6:6
We will endure suffering and reproach for Christ. Hebrews 11:26

Can you see what a lie Satan has perpetuated upon the Church? He is propagating a myth that thinking about heaven will make you of no earthly good. The Devil is propagating a lie that wanting heavenly reward will make you selfish, when in fact, thinking of heaven will do EXACTLY THE OPPOSITE. The prosperity gospel might make you selfish. The prosperity gospel might make you want things, material things now. But in the next life, when earth and heaven become one, all the things God gives us will not distract us from worship. Rather, his blessings will enhance worship. In this life, we turn God's blessings into idols (Deuteronomy 8:17). In the next life, without the presence of sin, we will enjoy all things in their proper place to the glory of God (Isaiah 25:6).

Imagine this endless circle of love; he gives, we receive, we cast back at his feet to honor him. That process will grow endlessly for eternity. And it will be a very physical, earthy, material experience with food, bodies, riches, land, mansions...all the things we are sinfully craving in this life we get in spades in the next life without the sinful, self-indulgent hangover effect!

---

[18] Über is German for "over," or "above." Colloquially we use the term for when something is over-the-top.

What? No one told me this. I thought we'd be floating around in clouds at a 1,000,000-year long church service.

Oh, and can you imagine, unlike American Idol where we glorify a singer exalting herself, God himself will sing over us (Zephaniah 3:17). I can't even begin to contemplate that scene. The pent up, frustrated dreams we have of singing for our own glory will be realized in perfection as we sing for Christ before an audience of millions and he turns around and sings to us (Zephaniah 3:14-17)!

Do you really think that this bowl of soup, this earthly existence is what we should set our hopes in? The American Dream? We are selling ourselves short. And I'm sorry to say, that the American Dream of achieving wealth and prosperity fails to live up to its promise. Does excessive materialism lead to joy? I don't think so. The American Dream without a kingdom purpose is a kingdom without a king.

> *Finally, there is laid up for me the crown of righteousness, which the Lord, the righteous Judge, will give to me on that Day, and not to me only but also to all who have loved His appearing. 2 Timothy 4:8*

Sin has so blinded us that instead of looking forward to Christ, instead of looking forward to heaven, we are filled with dread. We secretly hope he delays. We secretly hope he stays away. We secretly hope he never comes in this life. What sin! What a slap to his face that we don't hope to see our Savior! That we want to live a life of comfort and ease, take the path of least resistance, to NOT bring glory to his name in this life, to say a prayer and then live for ourselves, is that it?

The Church in America needs to deeply repent of this grievous sin. I need to deeply repent, because I am prone to wander, prone to misplace my hope, prone to slip and fall into placing my affections on earthly things. I need to repent and so do you.

In God's economy, God puts massive incentives in front of the Church in order to complete the Great Commission. Here's what I want you to meditate about: These rewards are real. They are not mere symbols, notional, fictitious types of rewards. They are more real than all the rusting houses and cars we possess. And believe it or not, if you hope in your heavenly treasure, you will live in a manner that is pleasing to the Lord.

Part 2

Equity: Your Heavenly Treasure

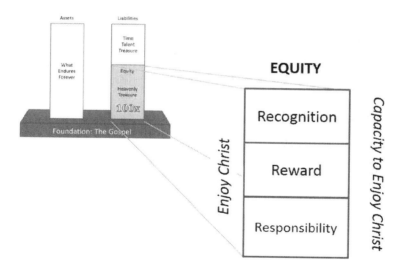

Chapter 4 – EQUITY – Your Birthright
Your heavenly treasure is better

*...lest there be any fornicator or profane person like Esau, who for one morsel of food **sold his birthright**. Hebrews 12:16*

In order to grow heavenly treasure you have to value things properly. Every day you are comparing the things of this world with the things of heaven and you are deciding what you value with your time, talent, and earthly treasure. The Bible uses comparative words like "better" and "greater" in order to help us make these decisions. Hebrews 11 goes into detail about the hall of heroes, story after story of people who endured, who lived for the glory of God, who hoped for a better city, a better reward.

> *By faith Moses, when he became of age, refused to be called the son of Pharaoh's daughter, choosing rather to suffer affliction with the people of God than to enjoy the passing pleasures of sin, **esteeming the reproach of Christ greater riches than the treasures in Egypt; for he looked to the reward**. Hebrews 11:24 – 26*

You see, when you have a better "yes" you can say "no" to all sorts of things. You can say "no" to a life that is devoted to comfort and ease. You can say "no" to a life that takes the path of least resistance. You can say "no" to sin that gives pleasure only for a season, but leaves you hollow and empty.

You can say "yes" to the joy set before you. You can say "yes" to a greater reward, a better inheritance, a better country, a better mansion. You can say "yes" to your birthright.

The absurdity of the story of Esau is that the birthright was of immeasurable worth. The bowl of soup that Jacob prepared for him satisfied him for only a few hours but the loss was incalculable. Despising your birthright means you look at the pleasures of this world and take not a thought for heaven. And when you don't care about your reward in heaven, you will live a life of sin. Sin creeps in and destroys you.

When I drive around Minnesota, I enjoy looking at the mansions that are built around the lakes. Listen, there's absolutely nothing wrong with having lakefront property. There's nothing wrong with living in a very large and nice house. I hope and pray that God blesses you to overflowing in a very material way. What is wrong is to put your hope in that. What is wrong is to sit on a boat, crack open a cold one, and say, "Life doesn't get any better than this." What is wrong is to take the blessings of God and love the gifts more than the Gift Giver. And when we love his "stuff" more than him, we are despising our birthright.

So when I drive around lakes surrounded by mansions, **I imagine a bowl of soup.**

Lord, how often does stuff and enjoying stuff get in my way of worshiping you? How often do I love things, care about things so much that I stop loving you and serving people? The more you buy, the more you have to maintain. The more you have to maintain, the more stuff sucks up your time. The more it takes your time, the more you worry that it's going to break. The more you worry it's going to break, the more you want to buy something better.

It's all soup.

Don't love soup more than your birthright.

You have a reward that is better, that is greater, and that is lovelier than the stuff of earth. You have a mansion with many rooms waiting for you. It's is bigger, more beautiful, more costly, more decked out than anything you could splurge on yourself in this life. You have treasure in knowing someone who calls you by name who is more important than kings, queens, potentates, presidents, prime ministers, and emperors. He is the king of the universe and he wants to know you and me intimately. What a treasure! What an absolute honor and privilege to spend life in pursuit of knowing him and making him known!

He is the prize. His glory and his fame are the prize. And when we live in such a way as to make him famous, we will say "no" to sin. We will live holy lives. We will live disciplined lives that avoid the excess of success and the fat of convenience. We will do hard things, difficult things because we are meant for more. We are meant for gold, eternal gold. It's ours for the taking. We are meant to stand on the victor's stand wearing a crown of glory. And on that day, all those who are rewarded with crowns will take off their crowns and cast them at his feet and fall prostrate before the Name above all Names (Revelation 4:10).

Your Inheritance
You can have it Now or Later

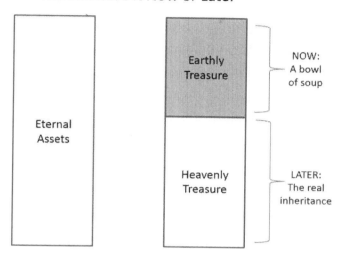

In God's economy, our Lord places in front of us unbelievably lavish incentives so that we might complete the Great Commission. We are constantly lured by the snare of the here and now, sin for a season. But the Bible tells us our equity in the next life is BETTER. The American Dream is nice. Our heavenly treasure is better. And if we truly believe that what is in store for us is infinitely better, we will press on through trials, tribulations, and suffering. We will joyfully forego some of the pleasures of this world, endlessly chasing the American Dream. We will produce the fruit of righteousness, and fulfill God's mission on earth.

Chapter 5 – EQUITY – Heavenly Treasure
The Equity Accounts of Recognition, Reward, and Responsibility

*How can you believe, who receive honor from one another, and **do not seek the honor that comes from the only God**? John 5:44*

Every eternal incentive is mirrored by what is offered to us today. Incentives fall into three buckets: recognition, reward, and responsibility. Recognition is the positive feeling you receive when someone of stature acknowledges your contribution. Reward is the material aspect where the amount of the value you generate is compensated with commensurate value. Responsibility is the acknowledgement that all of the value you create makes you fit for greater tasks. In heaven, God will render to our equity account all three as recompense.

Recognition
"Well done, good and faithful servant!" Matthew 25:21a

The first equity account is the most important account of them all. Recognition is God's approval. The prideful person will emphatically state that he does what is right because it's the right thing to do. Sounds pious, sounds lofty, but such a statement hides the seed of self-righteousness that elevates the approval of man over God. When we read scripture, we read that Jesus himself was motivated by his heavenly Father's approval. Recognition by God himself should be the chief motivator of all we do in this life. Wanting to please our heavenly Father is fundamental to loving God.

God designed us to long for and crave recognition. We can scarcely do a single good deed without wanting someone to pat us on the back. Every time I wash the dishes and my wife says nothing, I get upset, sometimes angry. "I'm busting my hump every day to put bread on the table. And on top of all of this, I'm helping out with the dishes!" I think to myself. My wife likes to joke that she has a box of gold star stickers to place on my chest to placate me. For some reason, God designed us with this need for recognition. We will either want it from man or from God. Jesus knew that. Jesus looked into the hearts of the religious leaders and saw past the façade of self-righteousness.

> *I do not receive honor from men. But I know you, that **you do not have the love of God in you.** I have come in my Father's name, and*

*you do not receive me; if another comes in his own name, him you will receive. How can you believe, who receive honor from one another, and **do not seek the honor that comes from the only God**? John 5:41 – 44*

You see, just like you cannot serve God and Mammon (money), you cannot seek recognition from both God and man. The Apostle Paul goes as far as to say that if you seek to please man you are not Christ's servant (Galatians 1:10).

The reason why we crave recognition is because we are made for glory. Glory demands display and demands praise. When you watch a pianist play flawlessly or a pitcher pitch a perfect game, you and the crowd cannot help but stand up and praise. Praise is the essence of recognition. It is calling things out for what they are. We exult in that which is beautiful, excellent, awesome, and worthy.

We were created to reflect the glory of God for the glory of God. Adam's sin was primarily about stealing God's glory by setting up man to be the ultimate arbiter of good and evil. We could decide for ourselves because of our god-like intellect. We've been patting ourselves on the backs ever since. Our greatest sin is not that we do bad things. Our greatest sin, the sin that condemns us to hell, is that **we think very highly of ourselves and not highly of God**, so much so that we ignore and transgress his laws. We value our glory. We devalue God's glory.

And so you see that the desire for recognition is ultimately about elevating self above God. "Look at me! Look at me!" We get incensed, offended, and insulted when someone at an awards ceremony mistakenly overlooks or forgets to recognize our accomplishments, right? In fact, it infuriates us. Deep down our pride is wounded. Why? Because glory demands display and we exalt our own glory above the glory of God.

That is why to desire God's recognition is ultimately the most humble posture a human could take. You have to suppress the desire for accolades, for titles, for your name in the spotlight here on earth. You have to be content with being someone behind the scenes and not resent it. And, ultimately your heavenly Father will recognize everything you've faithfully done in his name. He won't omit a single detail. He will lavish his affection and approval upon you in the presence of one hundred million angels.

In our heavenly treasure we are promised God's recognition. And if we long for his recognition in the next life, we will do all God requires in this life. The basis of courageous and outrageous feats of service for humanity is justification. Some people confuse this with trying to "earn" God's approval. We start with God's acceptance because Christ perfectly fulfilled all God's righteous requirements. Our fruit authenticates the deep roots of faith that spring from the power of Christ's perfect work. Christ's work merits God the Father saying to Jesus, "This is my beloved Son in whom I am well pleased." Through faith this gets passed on to us as, "Well done, good and faithful servant."

I love it when my children draw or paint something and run up to me, "Daddy, Daddy, look at what I drew for you!" This is what Jesus is referring to when he said that we must come to him like a little child (Matthew 18:3), with that pure longing for our heavenly Father's approval. Something tends to happen as we get older in the faith. We care less about our heavenly Father's approval. We may feel a little undignified to run to him. But dying on a cross is undignified and that did not stop Jesus. Yes, our thinking must mature and we must put *childish ways* behind us, as the Apostle Paul states (1 Corinthians 13:11). But we must maintain that childlike posture of longing and affection for God's approval.

If we want our heavenly treasure to grow, we must want God's approval. We must follow Jesus' example where our Lord himself did everything to please his heavenly Father. The highest praise is to hear, "Well done, good and faithful servant!" That alone should motivate us to go all out for the gospel.

Reward

Worthy is the Lamb who was slain, **to receive power and riches** and wisdom, and strength and honor and glory and blessing!" Revelation 5:12

In God's economy, he promises us an awful lot. Since what he promises seems so over the top, it would be tempting to view all of the reward as merely symbolic. The consequence of viewing heavenly reward as symbolic is that earthly reward then feels more real, and hence, more enticing. John Lennon sang about imagining that there was no money. Wouldn't a world without money be great? And yet, in Revelation 5, all creation declares to Christ that he is worthy to receive riches. That's odd. Yet if we truly understand what currency is, simply a unit to measure value, then we will rejoice that God promises us an abundance of heavenly currency in the next life.

Luke Chapter 16 gives us one of the most curious stories in the Bible, called the Parable of the Shrewd Manager. The Shrewd Manager (*oikonomian*) realizes that the master is going to demand an account of his dealings. He has heretofore been frivolous and wasteful with his master's business. He realizes that the jig is up and so he immediately starts collecting on his master's outstanding debts. Rather than write off the debts as a total loss, he is able to quickly give the master 50% - 80% of what is owed.[19] You might be thinking, "Hey, in the Parable of the Talents the master is angry that the servant with one talent produces only one talent. In this, the Shrewd Manager delivers half and is commended. What's going on?"

In God's Economy, the Lord bases our workmanship on two vectors: 1) current trajectory and 2) realized potential. What I mean is this: in this parable, the current trajectory of the Shrewd Manager was a total loss, 100% of everything in his care. The manager "repented," had a change of mind, and changed his trajectory. And in the short time remaining, he maximized his master's gains. We even see this in the American economy for debt collections. Banks will often write off bad debt completely or receive pennies on the dollar. Debt collection agencies will make a profit spread buying the debt for pennies on the dollar and then collecting on the debt, which can be 25% - 30%. A 50% collection would be a gigantic return on investment!

In the same way, many people look at the past and all the time they've wasted away not living for God. They would've, should've, could've lived for the kingdom but didn't. Too many people resign themselves to not doing anything and giving back to the master the one talent. (By the way, giving back one talent is a zero percent return.)

Other people, quickened by the Holy Spirit, get a wake-up call and for whatever time is left in their lives maximize the time remaining for the LORD. This is to be commended. And so Jesus goes on to say:

> *He who is faithful in what is least is faithful also in much; and he who is unjust in what is least is unjust also in much. Therefore if you have not been faithful in the unrighteous mammon, **who will commit to your trust the true riches**? And if you have not been faithful in*

---

[19] In John MacArthur's sermon (date 01-15-06), he interprets that the Shrewd Manager embezzles the master on his way out. When I compare and contrast Luke 16:1 ("this man was wasting his goods") with v.8 ("the master commended the unjust steward because he had dealt shrewdly") it doesn't make sense why the master would commend the Shrewd Manager for stealing from him. Nevertheless, the punch line of the story is the same: Money does not last. People last forever. Luke 15 – Luke 16:13 are part of one narrative. Jesus gives three parables (lost sheep, lost coin, lost son) to emphasize "lost people matter." He then transitions to the Shrewd Manager to emphasize "use money to win lost people who will welcome you in heaven." In God's economy, temporary wealth converts into true wealth through missions and evangelism.

*what is another man's, who will **give you what is your own**? Luke 16:10 -12*

Isn't it striking that Jesus promises **"true riches"** and **"what is your own?"** Using the eternal balance sheet as a guide, your liability accounts in this life (time, talent, and treasure) are God's investment in you. They are temporary and don't belong to you. You, by God's grace, apply yourself to maximize a kingdom return (eternal assets) and God gives you what is truly your own in the next life. This is awesome.

The Parable of the Shrewd Manager

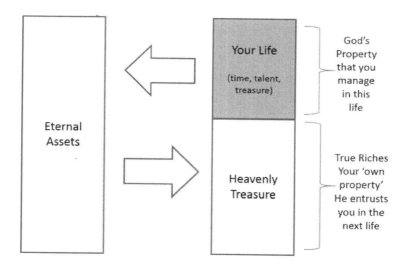

So you might be scratching your head because you're playing the John Lennon song in your mind. "I thought there was no money in heaven?" Why does the Bible talk about true riches?

Let me simplify what riches are. Money is unitized value, that's all. Unitizing value allows us to value things properly. *"Where your treasure is, there your heart will be also" (Matthew 6:21).* Unitizing value allows us to evaluate what is worthy and what is not. Why does Jesus illustrate God's forgiveness as paying a 10,000 talent debt, or the equivalent of $9

BILLION[20] (Matthew 18:24)? Because without unitizing value, we would have no clue how costly a sacrifice the cross represents and hence our emotions would be flat with no gratitude.[21] Unitizing value allows us to ratchet up our affections in proportion to the worth of the sacrifice.

Here's the shocker that is replete in the Bible. Riches are not going away. Earthly riches will indeed fail and fade. But heavenly riches exist and endure. And the faithful steward will receive from Christ recompense, payment, reward.

> *I counsel you to* **buy from me gold** *refined in the fire,* **that you may be rich**; *and white garments, that you may be clothed, that the shame of your nakedness may not be revealed; and anoint your eyes with eye salve, that you may see. Revelation 3:18*

In the book of Revelation, we see the Church in Laodicea in a deplorable condition. She has lost her first love and has followed the ways of the world. Rather than produce works that are either hot or cold, this church demonstrates a lukewarm attitude. They've become comfortable with their earthly riches. John sees a vision of Christ the King urging this church to **trade up earthly riches for heavenly riches**. History seems to indicate they failed to heed the warning and the Church in Laodicea no longer exists. God removed their lampstand. Sadly, Christians today are similar to the church in Laodicea and think very little of heavenly riches. Earthly riches feel so real. That car smells and feels so real. Granite kitchen counter tops feel so real. We fail to trade up for heavenly riches.

I know what you're thinking, "David, David, do you mean we'll have a bank account in heaven?" I don't know. What the Bible teaches is that the essence of the currency of heaven is joy. Read the passages on heavenly treasure[22] and you will read about much rejoicing, joy in heaven, leaping for

---

[20] A talent is the equivalent of 6000 drachmas. One drachma is approximately one day's wages. If we use 300 days as equaling one year's pay, then one talent equals 20 year's wages. 10,000 talents equals 200,000 years' worth of wages. Using $45,000 average annual salary, we multiply 45,000 x 200,000 = $9B. That sum would even be higher if we equated the talent using the gold standard. One talent equals approximately 33 kilograms which equal approximately 1061 troy ounces. At $1287 per oz., 10,000 talents equates to approximately $13.7B. In either case, Jesus is saying that our sin debt is an infinite cost that no one can pay. His blood, his sacrifice is of infinite value.

[21] Indeed, we tend to be more emotional about food, football, and fun than salvation. Our apparent lack of gratitude points to our lack of appreciation of the sheer value of the sacrifice.

[22] Verses where I equate joy with heavenly currency: Matthew 5:12, Luke 15:7, Luke 15:9, and most specifically, Matthew 13:44, "Again, the kingdom of heaven is like treasure hidden in a field, which a man found and hid; and **for joy over** it he goes and **sells all that he has** and buys that field."

joy, entering into joy. While I can't tell you the exact form of heavenly riches, what I deduce from all the scriptures is that heavenly riches represent the capacity to enjoy God and show forth his glory.

Equity Account

	Recognition	
Being with Christ	Reward	Capacity to Enjoy Christ
	Responsibility	

What many of you will struggle with as you contemplate heavenly riches is this tautology: "How can I have more of the infinite? If God is our treasure, does this mean I have more of God?" No. Our equity is a two-sided coin. On one side is the very presence of God. On the other side of the coin is the capacity to enjoy him.[23] We should want as much capacity as he will grant us.

So is it greedy to want heavenly riches? Quite the opposite! To grow heavenly treasure, *"He must increase and I must decrease"* (John 3:30). What is crazy about American Christians is that when it comes to earthly treasure, we act like capitalists. When it comes to heavenly treasure, we act like communists. We think everyone gets the same reward. And because we are indifferent to heavenly treasure we spend all of our earthly resources on our glory, our reputation, our stuff, our life experiences, and our possessions. Everything that is not for the glory of God will spoil and fade. If everything that endures is for the glory of God, then we should want as much resource, as much capacity as God will entrust us to extend the praise of his glory. Not only will this go to the ends of the earth, but to the ends of the universe (Ephesians 1:22).

---

[23] I did not come up with this concept of heavenly treasure equating to the capacity of joy on my own. This largely comes from my reading of Jonathan Edwards, C.S. Lewis, and John Piper.

Responsibility

*His lord said to him, 'Well done, good and faithful servant; you were **faithful over a few things, I will make you ruler over many things.** Enter into the joy of your lord. Matthew 25:21*

Because God put our work under a curse in this life, it's easy to think of work as a curse. Work is not a curse. Work is how God created the world in six days. He only rested on the seventh! And, in the amazing mystery of God's divine providence, he created us to be image bearers, to work and create something beautiful and reflect his glory.[24] In the next life, work will be brought out of the curse and our work will continue, forever.

So those who do this well in the life that is now will get amplified responsibilities in the life that is to come. Those who create order out of chaos, bring the best in others, provide purpose, direction, and meaning for productive ends will get more opportunities to multiply that in the next life. Our reward in the next life isn't rest and relaxation; it's more work!

Life won't be under curse. We won't toil in the sweat of our brow and watch our work crumble under the second law of thermodynamics[25]. Our work will grow and endure to the glory of God! Think of how meaningful work motivates people. Why? Because, *"My Father is working until now, and I am working" (John 5:17).* God the Father instituted the pattern in the six-days working, one-day resting creation narrative. Work existed before the Fall! Sin made work, grueling work.

When people contemplate a heaven without work, they lose motivation to go to heaven. Heaven without work seems so unbelievably boring. Part of the good news is that we were not just created for fellowship, we were created to rule. We will rule and reign with him, administering the kingdom to the ends of the earth and beyond (2 Timothy 2:12, Ephesians 1:22-23). The government will be upon his shoulders (Isaiah 9:6), and the Church will rule at his side (Revelation 20:4). Our hearts should race with excitement to think that this life is but a foretaste of glory divine. Our joining God's work makes work even more fulfilling.

---

[24] The common evangelical narrative is that God created us for "fellowship," almost like God was lonely. In Genesis 1:26-28, and Genesis 2 we read that man was created to rule, to multiply, tend the garden and name the creatures. Three of those four are work. One is for enjoyment/procreation. All are worship.

[25] The second law of thermodynamics simple states that everything tends to go from a state of order to disorder. It is also known as the law of entropy. Anyone with young children will know exactly what the law of entropy looks like. Thirty minutes after cleaning your house, your children will very vividly show what going from "order to disorder" looks like.

This is why the concept of retirement is antithetical to being a Christian. Our goal in life is not to cease from working and enter into endless self-indulgent recreation. Our goal in this life is to join God's work to advance the gospel. In this life, that work will end when we die or when the Lord returns. Rest and recreation are meant to rejuvenate us so that we can continue on with the mission and not grow weary.

Will you enter into that work now, while it is still day? Will you work to advance the gospel and his kingdom? Will you give everything so that the name of Jesus Christ is exalted from sea to shining sea? Will you use your time, talent, and treasure to make him famous? Everything you do for his glory will get credited to your account and you will be rewarded with 100x the responsibility to extend his glory to the ends of the universe.[26]

---

[26] In Ephesians 1:17 – 23, Paul writes that God exalts Christ to the right hand of God in the heavenly places for the Church, fullness of him who fills all in all. Since we are finite beings, I deduce that our filling all in all will mean that we will explore the universe throughout eternity. In Romans 8:18 – 25, all of creation is waiting for the sons of God to be revealed. In 2 Peter 3:10, all heaven will pass away, and be remade. (Revelation 21:1) So from God remaking the entire universe to be fit for the Church to rule, I conclude that it will take a very LONG time for creation to see the sons of God revealed, but we'll have a long time ahead of us.

Chapter 6 – EQUITY – There's Gonna Be a Reckoning
The Great Reversal

"But many who are first will be last, and the last first." Matthew 19:30
"He will judge the world with righteousness, and the peoples with equity."
Psalm 98:9

If Christ absorbs the wrath of God so there is no condemnation for those who are in Christ Jesus, what then is the whole point of God's judgment? Why is he going to judge anyone? Aren't we all going to get the same thing anyway? Modern Christians have so distorted grace that many have completely neglected to understand that God is the ultimate, perfect judge. Where no justice prevails in this world, he will set all things straight in the next life. The equity account in the eternal balance sheet provides an illustration of how this is so.

As I was studying for my CFA exams, I went to a crash course in Dallas. The instructor was going over the balance sheet and said, "This is the most important equation you will ever memorize. **Assets minus Liabilities equal Equity.**" What he meant was that wealth is the remainder of everything you produce minus everything it took to produce the wealth. This simple equation reveals why there are Americans who can make $100k per year in income and still not have net wealth. Why? Because they might have lots of assets in the form of cars, houses, and jewelry, but the amount of debt they use to finance their lavish living leaves them with very little equity, or net wealth.

<u>Assets minus liabilities equal equity</u>. Equity is what keeps everything fair and in balance. If the balance sheet is not in balance, equity takes the hit until the equation rebalances. In this way we can start to understand certain scriptures about how God's perfect judgment will unfold. Let's start with the story most of us are familiar with, the Parable of the Talents.

> *"For it will be like a man going on a journey, who called his servants and **entrusted to them his property**. To one he gave **five talents**, to another **two**, to another **one**, to each according to his ability. Then he went away. He who had received the five talents **went at once and traded** with them, and he made five talents more. So also he who had the two talents made two talents more. But he who had received the one talent went and dug in the ground and **hid his master's money**.*

*Now after a long time the master of those servants came and **settled accounts** with them. And he who had received the five talents came forward, bringing five talents more, saying, 'Master, you delivered to me five talents; here I have made five talents **more.**' His master said to him, '**Well done**, good and faithful servant. You have been faithful over a little; I will set you over much. **Enter into the joy** of your master.' Matthew 25:14-21*

The first thing I want to note, and I hope this is not lost on us are the words, "entrusted to them **his property**." In order for us to enter into the joy of building up our heavenly treasure, we must first look at this earthly treasure as a loan. Our money, homes, our reputations, and our stuff are his property, all of it. We own nothing. If we just believe that, the rest of this book is quite easy to comprehend. The principle of stewardship is that we are like management of a public company. Think of God's economy like Apple Inc. He owns the most valuable piece of property on the planet and is asking you to take it to the next level.[27] He's giving you stock options[28] that vest when you produce more fruit beyond what you've been given. And so, motivated to grow this awesome enterprise, you commit yourself to being more innovative, working harder, to sacrificing more for your equity piece of the pie. Now that would be true for the CEO all the way down to someone in the warehouse who was also given stock options. The HOPE for the upside of the equity motivates us in the here and now to produce FRUIT, innovation, hard work, excellence. God owns all of it. We manage it. We enjoy the upside.

The second thing I would like to note is that everyone is given something, according to his ability. The Greek word used is "dynamos" or "power." "Dynamos" is a grace gift. Nothing we are born with in this world is deserved. God accords that ability purely according to his grace. Why were you and I born in America? How fair is that? Why did God give us so much "dynamos?" Not because we're better than people born in other parts of the world. He's testing us to see what we'll do with that "dynamos" once he puts money, or talents in our hands. It's all grace.

---

[27] In equity markets, we see a phenomenon known as "principal-agent conflict." Management, even though they own equity, many times are not aligned with the owner's interests. Management use the owner's capital to indulge themselves to the shareholders' detriment. In God's economy, we are managers and God is the owner. We see "principal-agent conflict" as Christians indulge themselves using God's resources for pleasure and personal glory rather than the Great Commission.

[28] Technically, it more resembles a callable, convertible bond. Time, talent, and treasure are a loan that God can call back at any time. By meeting certain thresholds that bond converts into equity – probably too financial a concept for this book, but someday I will write about why this financial structure actually produces the best outcomes.

The third thing I would like to note is that the productive servants all *doubled* their money.[29] God rewards excellence. God expects results. God expects real fruit, not just effort. He wants a 100% return on his investment. God's people are a reflection on his reputation. So we can't produce shoddy results at work. Even if we collect a paycheck we are to work as unto the Lord. This is why unemployment destroys human dignity. We were made to work and produce fruitfulness. Why? Because he wants to reward us with our inheritance and stay true to his nature, which not only reflects lavish grace, but is also full of justice and equity. The mercy of God absorbs the wrath of God. The grace of God ushers us into eternal life. The justice and equity of God reward us according to the fruit we produce in this life. The eternal balance sheet illustrates the Parable of the Talents.

The Parable of the Talents
The productive servant

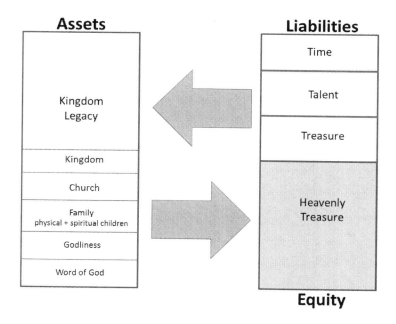

---

[29] Even though the unit of money is called a "talent," Jesus was talking about money. Many people gloss over this fact and think of this parable more in terms of serving in the church and ignore the money question, like money belongs to a different kingdom. The eternal balance sheet ties time, talent, and treasure into one big liability bucket. In other words, we are to invest ALL that God gives us and hold nothing back.

Notice in verse 19, "the master of those servants came and _**settled accounts**_ with them." I want to highlight the words "settled accounts" because people will look at this balance sheet illustration and think, "I hate these bean-counters, always trying to make the numbers work." Proverbs 11:1 says, "A false balance is an abomination to the LORD, but a just weight is his delight." None of us are each other's judge. Our own appraisal system is completely messed up because of our sin. I'm not saying I know exactly how God's accounting system works, but in God's perfection, he will judge the world with his own accounting system that includes thoughts, words, and deeds.

> _I, the LORD, search the heart,_
> _I test the mind,_
> _Even to give every man according to his ways,_
> _According to the fruit of his doings. Jeremiah 17:10_

The Master will settle accounts. Thinking about this should simultaneously fill us with both hope and terror, but we trust that our heavenly Father is not only just, but full of grace.

Return on Investment

I invite you to get to know certain organizations where the return on investment is huge. The more I spend time learning about the kind of pastors and missionaries that our emerging world churches train and the fruit they produce, I am completely humbled. The proportionate fruit these pastors, missionaries, and lay leaders are producing relative to the paucity and scarcity of money they are given astounds and humbles me. They live on $2 per day! And I think about our God who is perfectly just and perfectly equitable. In this life, they didn't get all the resources, "dynamos" that I was given, but oh in the next life will they receive their reward!

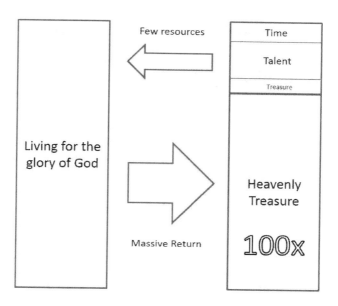

God is telling us to store up our treasure in heaven. And here's what blows my mind. Your piece of the equity can be as big as you want it to be.

> *Give, and it will be given to you. Good measure, pressed down, shaken together, running over, will be put into your lap. For **with the measure you use** it will be measured back to you.   Luke 6:38*

Now for the great reversal: God gives everyone something to invest. He expects a return.

> *He also who had received the one talent came forward, saying, 'Master, I knew you to be a hard man, reaping where you did not sow, and gathering where you scattered no seed, so I **was afraid**, and I went and **hid** your talent in the ground. Here you have what is yours.' But his master answered him, 'You wicked and slothful servant! You knew that I reap where I have not sown and gather where I scattered no seed? **Then you ought to have invested my money with the bankers**, and at my coming I should have received what was my own with interest. So take the talent from him and give it to him who has the ten talents. For to everyone who has will **more be given**, and he will have an **abundance**. But from the one who has not, even what he has will be taken away. And cast the **worthless** servant into the outer darkness. In that place there will be weeping and gnashing of teeth.' Matthew 25: 24-30*

Only that which lasts for eternity will accrue to our asset account. The time we invest in the Word of God, the time we spend meditating and praying, the time we invest in becoming more Christ-like[30], the time we spend discipling our family and children, the time and talent we invest in serving others in the Church, the money we invest in supporting our church, the money we invest in supporting kingdom causes, the time and passion we spend loving God and others; all of those will be rewarded in the last day. Do you know why people rush through their quiet time in 15 minutes and then scurry to get to work where they lavish all of their productive capacity? They misjudge what generates a return on investment. The great reversal is when God reveals what we did that endures for eternity and what we did that was a frivolous waste.

> *Now if anyone builds on the foundation with gold, silver, precious stones, wood, hay, straw—each one's work will become manifest, for the Day will disclose it, because it will be revealed by fire, and the fire will test what sort of work each one has done. If the work that anyone has built on the foundation survives, he will receive a reward. If anyone's work is burned up, he will suffer loss, though he himself will be saved, but only as through fire. 1 Corinthians 3:12-15*

Can there be negative equity?

I think it's going to shock many people who had every advantage in this life, every resource humanly possible given to them. Those who squander all of God's gifts will be shocked to learn that God does not look kindly on squandering his resources.[31] His scales are perfect. His judgments are perfect. His weights are perfect and he expects a return. Just to use accurate language, break-even is when your inputs equal your outputs and there is no profit. A loss is when your output is less than your input. That's negative profit. So, even in the Parable of the Talent you might confuse yourself to think that one talent in minus one talent out is breakeven. But remember, we are given time and ability as well.
By illustration, I show below that one unit of treasure in producing one unit of treasure out completely fails to take into account time and ability (human

---

[30] Christ-likeness manifested at work, at home, and at play. We have to stop being different people in different settings. Integrity means to bring together to one unified whole. In contrast, we live lives of duplicity, acting in silos.

[31] Jesus contrasts two servants who totally maximized their talents and one who did nothing. The one who did nothing revealed himself to be a false servant and was sent to hell. Our works reveal and authenticate our faith. However, works do not equal faith, meaning it would be wrong to reverse the equation and "do more" to "prove" you are a Christian. Faith comes first. Most of us are somewhere in between the five talent servant and the one talent servant.

talent). God expects us to maximize all three. And in fact, that Master scolds the foolish servant that even a person with a **minimum of talent** would have used the **time** value of money to produce some interest bearing **profit**.

Parable of the Talents
The foolish servant with one talent

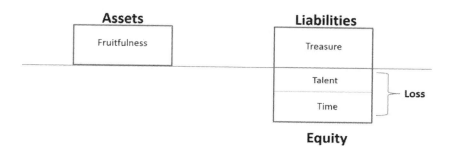

The Great Reversal happens when God takes the treasure not invested for the kingdom from those who had it in this life, and then hands all that treasure to those who produced the most for his glory. So, all those wonderful pastors, missionaries, lay-leaders who are *effectively* planting churches, making disciples around the world on $400 per year, I can only imagine and smile when I think of the treasure awaits them.

As for many of us in America... the more I study about God's perfect and equitable judgments, I start to understand why the Bible says, "the fear of the Lord is the beginning of wisdom" (Proverbs 1:7). He is so terrifyingly perfect, so just, so fair in his assessments. Do we in America think we're going to skate by in luxury and excess and be rewarded for that? Do we despise our heavenly treasure that much?

In America, we are first in this life. Don't be surprised if we are last in the life to come.

But many who are first will be last, and the last first. Matthew 19:30

Producing Wood, Hay, and Stubble

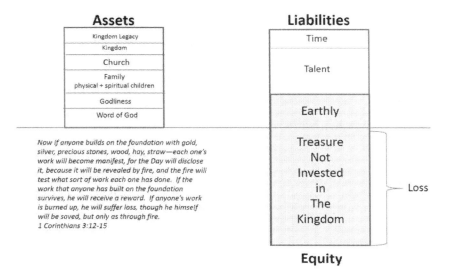

Assets

Kingdom Legacy
Kingdom
Church
Family physical + spiritual children
Godliness
Word of God

Now if anyone builds on the foundation with gold, silver, precious stones, wood, hay, straw—each one's work will become manifest, for the Day will disclose it, because it will be revealed by fire, and the fire will test what sort of work each one has done. If the work that anyone has built on the foundation survives, he will receive a reward. If anyone's work is burned up, he will suffer loss, though he himself will be saved, but only as through fire.
1 Corinthians 3:12-15

Liabilities

Time
Talent
Earthly
Treasure Not Invested in The Kingdom

— Loss

Equity

I think in America we overestimate how much fruit we are producing. We are very generous to ourselves in our own estimation. In America, we have been entrusted with TRILLIONS of dollars of earthly treasure and many of us think we are poor! Simultaneously, we are pretty proud of what our wealth buys. We exalt in our large screen TVs, our houses, our cars, our reputation, and our resumes. We are constantly comparing ourselves to others. What is mind-boggling is that American Christians possess almost all the wealth in Christendom.

> *For you say, I am rich, I have prospered, and I need nothing, **not realizing** that you are wretched, pitiable, **poor**, blind, and naked. I counsel you to buy from me gold refined by fire, so that you may be rich, and white garments so that you may clothe yourself and the shame of your nakedness may not be seen, and salve to anoint your eyes, so that you may see.   Revelation 3:17-18*

And,

> *But I have this against you, that you have **abandoned the love you had at first**. Remember therefore from where you have fallen; repent, and do the works you did at first. If not, I will come to you and*

remove your lampstand *from its place,* **unless you repent.**
Revelation 2:4-5

What does it look like to have your lampstand removed on a church level? Well, go to Laodicea and Ephesus in Turkey. You won't find vibrant, spiritual congregations there. There are only ruins. As much as I love America, just because we say things like "God Bless America" does not mean we are in a right standing with him. No church on a country level has survived being prosperous, not one in the 2,000 year history of the Church. We may already be post-Christian where the entire society, the basis of our legal system is completely rejecting a Judeo-Christian framework. And if the foundations are destroyed, what can the righteous do (Psalm 11:3)?

In God's economy there's coming a day of reckoning, not of condemnation, but of reward. In justification, we pass from death to life and are invited to participate in God's redemptive work. God will recompense us according to all the fruit we produce based on all the gifts he has given us. He has given the Church in America enough resources to complete the Great Commission many times over. What we lack are not resources. We lack faith. We lack obedience. We are exulting in our bloated excess wealth and someday there's gonna' be a reckoning.

Part 3

Assets: What Endures Forever

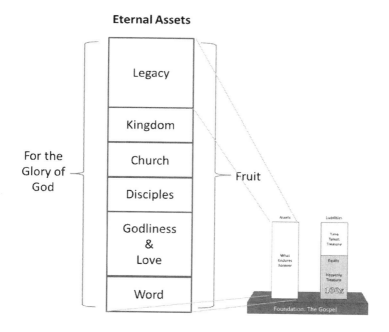

Chapter 7 – ASSETS – Overview
Working for that which endures

*Do **not work** for the food that **perishes**, but for the food that **endures to eternal life**, which the Son of Man will give to you. For on him God the Father has set his seal." John 6:27*

We have but one life to live and none of us knows how much time on this earth we have. So for all of us who are called to Christ, who are justified freely by his blood, who are adopted as heirs to his kingdom, he has work for us to do. What is that work? That work is more than our day jobs, more than just getting our kids to college. We are to increase our fruit in that which endures forever, everything God deems valuable. And what God deems most valuable is the glory of his name.

When we finish strong, we receive God's commendation.

> *I have fought the good fight, I have finished the race, I have kept the faith. Finally, there is laid up for me the crown of righteousness, which the Lord, the righteous judge, will give to me on that day, and not to me only but also to all who have loved his appearing. 2 Timothy 4: 7-8*

Finishing well will impact your heavenly treasure far more than starting well. That is why there are no verses in the Bible that commend starting strong but limping to the finish line. If we want to store up treasures in heaven, we will invest all of our time, talent, and treasure toward that which endures forever.

What does the Bible say endures forever?

His steadfast love endures forever	Psalm 106:1
God's righteousness endure forever	Psalm 111:3
The name of the Lord endures forever	Psalm 135:13
His kingdom endures forever	Psalm 145:13
Children of God belong to God's house forever	John 8:35
The saints will possess the kingdom forever	Daniel 7:18

The Word of God endures forever   Isaiah 40:8

We are to work for that which endures forever, because those things are valuable to God. He designed all the aforementioned to stand the test of time. When we are aligned with God's purpose to grow and nurture that which endures, we bring glory to our heavenly Father.

If we are to work for fruit that endures forever, let's take the opposite approach. <u>What does not endure forever</u>? What will we get no credits for? What earns a profit of ZERO?

> Whenever we work for the glory of our name, our fame, **our own personal advancement and reputation** earns a profit of ZERO. 1 Corinthians 10:13
>
> Whenever **we take credit for our accomplishments** instead of giving God the glory, earns a profit of ZERO. Isaiah 42:8
>
> Whenever we are **ashamed of Jesus' name** because we care more what other people think of us earns a profit of ZERO. Philippians 2:9-11
>
> Whenever we give, pray, or fast to **enhance our own esteem in the eyes of others** earns a profit of ZERO. Matthew 6:4, 6
>
> Whenever we do things in a manner that is **not worthy of the gospel** earns a profit of ZERO. Philippians 1:21 – 28
>
> Whenever we **store up money and treasure on this earth** for ourselves earns a profit of ZERO. Matthew 6:19-20
>
> Whenever we **hoard the blessings of God** instead of distributing blessing earns a profit of ZERO. Proverbs 11:26
>
> Whenever **we only do good to those who can repay us** earns a profit of ZERO. Luke 6:33 – 43
>
> Whenever we do things **without love**, we earn a profit of ZERO. 1 Corinthians 13:3

When I say "profit of ZERO" what I am saying is that in those cases my fruit is rotten, I've received my reward in full, I get no credit, none of it accrues toward my heavenly treasure.

In fact, what we discover upon evaluating ourselves in the light of God's Word, is that we are wasting too much of our lives on things that will fade away. We toil away to build up our wealth, our reputation, and our homes but how much time do we spend on building God's kingdom?

> *If anyone's work which he has built on it endures, he will receive a reward. If anyone's work is burned, he will suffer loss; but he himself will be saved, yet so as through fire. 1 Corinthians 3:15*

We are saved by grace but created for works, the kind of work that endures. The reason why God's kingdom, God's people, and God's Word endure forever is because they are rooted in the infinite value of God's character and nature. So, when we join God's work, we are in fact declaring our worship to him.

Worship – Our Declaration of God's Worth

> *Give unto the LORD the glory **due** unto his name: **bring an offering**, and come into his courts. Psalm 96:8*

> *Give unto the LORD the glory **due** unto his name; **worship** the LORD in the beauty of holiness. Psalm 29:2*

> *You are **worthy**, O Lord, to **receive glory** and honor and power: for you have created all things, and for your pleasure they are and were created. Revelation 4:11*

> *Worthy is the Lamb, who was slain, to **receive** power and **wealth** and wisdom and strength and honor and glory and praise! Revelations 5:12*

Declaring back to God this appraisal, this valuation of his worth is called worship. When we see him with spiritual eyes, and correctly evaluate that there is no comparison between God and creation, that is worship. When we delight in seeing his value clearly, that is worship. Delight results in obedience, being a living sacrifice, which is also worship (Romans 12:1).

Worship is absolutely the most natural response a human being has toward seeing something "awesome." Observe a crowd of men at some sporting event. Their favorite athlete makes the impossible shot at the buzzer and wins the big game. What does everyone do? En masse they raise their arms and praise that athlete. This is spontaneous, automatic, unforced, joy producing worship. We can't help but worship those things that we deem are WORTHY of our praise.

So, what is absolutely sinful is to see God in his splendor and beauty and to 1) not give him credit for all the good he has done and 2) take the credit yourself or lavish the praise on something or someone else. Both are stealing God's glory, and both make God furious.

> *Professing to be wise, they became fools, and changed the glory of the incorruptible God into an image made like corruptible man...*
> *Romans 1: 22-23a*

Don't you get angry when someone takes your idea at work and pretends like he came up with it? Don't you get indignant when someone takes credit for something she had little to do with? We humans are offended in instances where we aren't given proper credit. How much more then should God be upset when we refuse to acknowledge him, when we steal glory from him?

In order to find our life's purpose, we must put all things in their proper place. Through the Holy Spirit's illumination as revealed in the Word of God, we see God's uniqueness. We see how mankind as a whole and individually have stolen his glory and usurped his kingship. We are guilty of being glory stealing rebels. When we respond to the gospel, we don't merely ask for forgiveness for sins. We ask the Holy Spirit to change our thinking (repentance – *metanoia*) so that we can see God as he really is. He is unique and set apart, all together one of a kind. HOLY, HOLY, HOLY.

The aspects of his holiness, his *set-apartness* that we can comprehend with our senses are called glory. When we see his glory we declare to him what we think of it. That is praise. And the entire act of aligning ourselves so that our whole lives are devoted toward amplifying his worthiness is worship. Getting others to see his glory is evangelism. And taking his glory to the ends of the earth is missions.

Why focus on the worthiness of Christ?

Worthy is the Lamb that was slain to receive power, and riches, and wisdom, and strength, and honour, and glory, and blessing. Revelations 5:12

In order to find your life purpose, you must first understand why Christ is worth all of your time, talent, and treasure. Here's the paradox of finding purpose. You don't find purpose by taking an assessment. I love taking different personality tests and strengths profiles. I'm a gifts assessment junkie. It's fascinating to triangulate the test results and imagine my perfect job. But here's the rub. You will not find your purpose by answering a questionnaire. You find your purpose by serving Christ, by converting your time, talent, and treasure into what endures for eternity.   Through that long faithful service, you will learn your purpose.

Look at Joseph[32]. His dreams were so crystal clear, so vivid, and so full of clarity, that he could recount his destiny to his parents and siblings. The visions made sense to him. He was meant to lead and rule. Others were meant to follow. Joseph was meant for greatness.

If Joseph acted like an American evangelical, his detour to prison in Egypt, and his long wait in that same prison would have destroyed his faith. Was this maximizing his talents? How dare God squander and waste Joseph's time in prison?

No, Joseph did not sit around thinking about purpose and how his gifts were squandered in a jail. He was faithful and fruitful in every circumstance, blessing his captors through his fruitfulness. That fruitfulness produced more fruit and more responsibility until God's purpose was ultimately revealed many years later. Pharaoh exalts Joseph to vice-regent of the kingdom, and Joseph saves his family from starvation.

Think about us. We lose heart so easily. We think God doesn't have a plan for us because it seems we are stuck in a dead-end job. Sometimes we feel we're missing out on our purpose when we see others living more exciting lives and we're doing the same mundane thing year after year. Or, we might be unemployed and the frustration of even finding a decent job, let alone a soul satisfying career, leaves us full of bitterness toward God. We might be single, longing to find the perfect mate. We might be "stuck" in a marriage that feels loveless. We might feel overwhelmed by our life stage, with kids, without kids, driving around to games, flying around on business trips. And

---

[32] Genesis Chapters 35 through 50

if we obsess too much with finding our purpose, we might miss out on our first assignment: Count Christ worthy of everything.

> *Yea doubtless, and I count **all things but loss** for the excellency of the knowledge of Christ Jesus my Lord: for whom I have suffered the loss of all things, and do **count them but dung**, that I may **win Christ**. Philippians 3:8*

One of the reasons why I believe God often leads us on a long, sanctifying goose chase of unfulfilled dreams is to get us to stop thinking about self. The highest cause in life is not self-fulfillment, but self-denial. Jesus was God but emptied himself of the glory of God and became a servant (Philippians 2:5–8). How's that for discovering your hidden talents?

In the American version of the successful Christian life, Jesus would have seemed like a failure. He didn't achieve much of a bucket list. He didn't chase "success first, then significance."[33] He went from obscurity to sudden fame to infamy and died a cruel death, hated by all. If we didn't believe in the resurrection, we would look on Jesus as a horrible example to follow. To not get married, have children, watch them graduate college, play with grandchildren, is Jesus really our role model? He said "I came not to be served but to serve?" I've been treated like a servant before and I tell you what, it's not something I enjoy.

What cures us from our narcissism and allows us to be free to serve others is focusing on Christ and his worthiness. He is worthy. Our savior lived a perfect life, fulfilled all of God's righteous requirements. He is worthy. Our savior died the death that we deserved. He is worthy. Our savior overturned the laws of physics when he rose again, when he defeated sin, hell, Satan, and death. He is worthy. He is so worthy that if I never get to live out all of my hidden dreams in this life, if I never get to check off my bucket list, if I never reach the zenith of goal accomplishment but know him as my Lord, it's all worth it.

When he sanctifies us and frees us from our relentless need to get our egos stroked, then, perhaps, he starts to open the doors to use our passions and talents for greater and greater impact.

---

[33] In the book, I will often use a phrase like, "success to significance." I am not at all referring to Bob Buford's book Halftime. I am aware he has registered the trademark *Moving from Success to Significance*®. What I hear in everyday conversations is this notion, this paradigm. The common man's use of the phrase "success to significance" means "I come first, then someday before I die I'll start to think about eternal significance."

I like the story that evangelist Greg Laurie tells about when he became a Christian. He felt in his heart, with great conviction, that he was meant to be a preacher. I'm sure he envisioned himself standing in front of thousands of people and seeing them respond to the gospel. So, he told this desire to his pastor, Chuck Smith. Chuck handed him a mop and told him to get to work and serve the church. In other words, none of us is so important that we can't be the servant of all. And, it took years for Greg Laurie to go from being a disciple himself to being one of the greatest evangelists of our time.

When we meditate on the truth of Christ's worthiness, here's how we should respond. *King Jesus, I want to be part of your kingdom advancement. Here am I. Use me. Send me. I'll mop the floors. I'll clean your kitchen. I'll wait on tables. I'll change diapers. I'll volunteer for Sunday School. I'll do any task for you King Jesus because you are worthy. Please use my five loaves and two fish. Please use my one talent, two talents, five talents. Grow me in sanctification. Grow me in maturity. Use me now. Increase my faithfulness and my fruitfulness.*

You see, Joseph had to be weaned off of his narcissism before he could rule God's way. God had to knock him off his personal pedestal and sanctify his ego so that he could lead and not be a tyrant. This took 13 years of God sifting, sanding, refining, and shaping Joseph in jail until he was ready to discover his purpose, unlock his talents, and live out his potential. Faithfulness precedes responsibility and impact.

Glory demands display

How can you believe, when you receive glory from one another and do not seek the glory that comes from the only God? John 5:44

I was at a kids' Christmas dance recital. We showed up 30 minutes in advance to get a seat. The parking lot was already jam packed. The parents and grandparents were shoulder to shoulder pressing in, jockeying for the door. When the door opened, parents and grandparents scrambled for the best seats to see the glory of their kids displayed. When the music started and their children fluttered and floated in front, parents and grandparents leaned in, to absorb every moment of the glory of their kids displayed. iPhones and cameras tracked the children's every movements so as to not miss one glorious moment. And oh the adulation and praise that went forth when their children took a bow at curtain call. Glory demands praise.

The most natural thing to do is to sing praises of that which we adore. Praise needs no coercion, needs no legalistic orders to induce a heartfelt response. We were made for praise.

So, when our hearts show a preference for created things above the Creator we are telling God how little we think of him. We are telling our Creator that his glory has no weight and that the weight of our glory requires us to lean in. We prefer the temporal things of this world. We prefer watching a large screen television to reading the Bible. We prefer watching grown men beat each other up on the gridiron to worshiping Christ. We prefer basking in the rays of the sun to basking in prayer. We long for earthly mansions with granite kitchen countertops more than we long for heavenly mansions.

We know this is true yet our hearts and our actions betray us.

> *The god of this age has blinded the minds of them who believe not, lest the light of the glorious gospel of Christ, who is the image of God, should shine unto them. 2 Corinthians 4:4*

One of the Devil's primary strategies to keep people from the gospel is to blind their minds. The more clearly we see Jesus Christ, who he is, what he did, in his glory, the more we will love him. Unfortunately the avenue to seeing the glory of Christ is not through natural eyes, but through spiritual eyes that discern scripture. That is why faith comes from hearing the message and the message through the Word of God (Romans 10:17). When the Holy Spirit peels off the scales from our eyes, we see what is truly beautiful, truly praiseworthy, and the things of this world lose their luster. But oh how we love the world's luster!

This is where the Devil tricks us. He takes those avenues of natural revelation, namely, all the glitter and glamor that we can see and touch, and causes us to be short sighted and spellbound. We cannot physically see our heavenly treasure. We can see our banking statements. We cannot see our mansions of glory but we can see our houses by the lake. It takes the special revelation of scripture, through the illumination of the Holy Spirit to connect the dots and not get stuck on only the things we can physically see. We all somehow fall short of the glory of God.

The purpose of our lives is to reflect the glory of God to all casual observers and most importantly to that audience of one, our heavenly Father. By living in a manner that shouts, "transformed by the gospel!" we glorify God. And we want that story to be as brilliant as possible, don't we?

We are empty jars of clay filled with the power of God. No one focuses on the vessel but on what is inside the vessel. When we want to draw attention to ourselves, we steal glory from God. When we live lives of such improbable joy and love in the midst of sorrow and suffering, our vessels point to the reality of the gospel. That is why the Bible says that in the midst of persecution and suffering we are "more than conquerors" (Romans 8:37). A courageous, victorious life makes people sit up and take notice.

If your life, if my life is a pass-through to seeing the glory of God, then I want my life, my family's life to be as glorious as possible, don't you?

Assets, Simplified

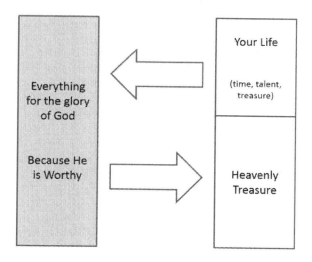

Thou art worthy, O Lord, to receive glory and honour and power: for thou hast created all things, and for thy pleasure they are and were created. Revelation 4:11 KJV

Chapter 8 – ETERNAL ASSETS – The Word of God

To get fruit, your roots have to go deeper

Study to show thyself approved unto God, a workman that needeth not to be ashamed, rightly dividing the Word of truth. 2 Timothy 2:15 KJV

I just finished a week of business travel to an oil and gas conference and guess what all the rage was? Horizontal fracking. Leaders in business and government from all over the world converged on Houston to ask themselves, "How can we take this shale revolution around the world?" Just a few years ago pundits were talking about the imminent decline in American power coupled with a persistent, massive annual import of oil. Now, America has its mojo back and the world is watching with wonder. Just like horizontal fracking has unleashed an unbelievable treasure of wealth and energy, we can draw from this illustration about how we can approach our biblical studies to find treasure in the Word of God.

Let's look at how we've typically approached Bible study. Think of study like conventional vertical oil drilling. We compartmentalize our lives by our age and life stage and approach the Bible looking for answers.

> *"How can I make the right choice as to which college to attend?"*
> *"How do I find the right person to marry?"*
> *"How do I become a better husband or wife?"*
> *"How do I become a better parent?"*
> *"How can I find purpose at work?"*
> *"How can I go from success to significance?"*

We structure all of church world in these silos. We have a marriage pastor, a pastor for families, a pastor for seniors, and a pastor for singles. We create programs around those silos, marriage encounters, parenting seminars, men's manly man-up weekends, father-daughter retreats, etc. We study specific scriptures about those particularly RELEVANT topics. We love that word, relevant. And so the way we interpret those scriptures is entirely contextual into our circumstance.

The same goes for when we look into scripture based on life events. Someone gets sick. Look for verses on healing. Someone feels scared. Look for verses on comfort. Your loved ones are traveling. Look for verses about safety and security. *"He who dwells in the shelter of the Most High..."* Check.

This even spills into how evangelicals pray. We say the word "just" a lot. Have you noticed that? *"I just ask for safety. I just ask you Lord for healing. I just ask that you comfort her. I just ask that you give me courage."* Inadvertently our words surface what's deep and hidden in many of our hearts. We don't want God to talk to us outside of what we "just" want to go to him for. Forget the Lord's agenda. I just want answers for what is relevant for me today.

And like the vertical drilling example, we read the Bible, we pray, we attend Sunday School until that well is dry and we move on. We go from well to well, seeking to extract just what we "just" need until we come to the twilight of our lives and we ask ourselves, "How do I move from success to significance?" We attend a few fund raisers, give some money and then go back on vacation. The well is dry.

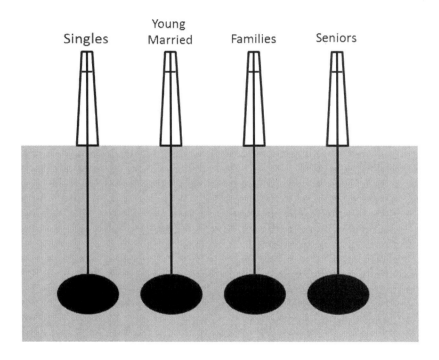

What we're missing is the mother lode, which is the entire meta-narrative of the gospel of the glory of God.

> *To me, though I am the very least of all the saints, this grace was given, to preach to the Gentiles the unsearchable riches of Christ, and to bring to light for everyone what is the plan of the mystery hidden for ages in God who created all things, so that through the church the manifold wisdom of God might now be made known to the rulers and authorities in the heavenly places. This was according to the eternal purpose that he has realized in Christ Jesus our Lord...*
> *Ephesians 3:8-11*

You see the gospel is not "just" about you getting saved by praying a prayer and then having God answer your timely questions. **The gospel is about God.** Through creation, fall, redemption, glorification, consummation, and future reign the gospel reveals the fullness of his glory. Through sin, death, pain, and suffering God reveals a marvelous tapestry of mind-boggling intricate beauty. And guess what? We are a part of all of it.

If you want the fullness of the treasure that is in scripture you have to drill deeper. An average vertical oil well is approximately 3,500 feet. The average horizontal frack well is 5,000 – 9,000 vertical feet. Equally amazing is that the well is drilled 10,000 feet *horizontally*. The mother lode is cutting across all the silos to get at the core of this massive treasure. In scripture what is this treasure? The treasure is the glory of God.

> *Oh, the **depth of the riches** both of the **wisdom and knowledge of God**! How unsearchable are his judgments and his ways past finding out! "For who has known the mind of the Lord? Or who has become his counselor?" Or "who has first given to Him and it shall be repaid to him?"*
>
> *For of Him and through Him and to Him are all things, **to whom be glory forever. Amen.** Romans 11: 33-36*

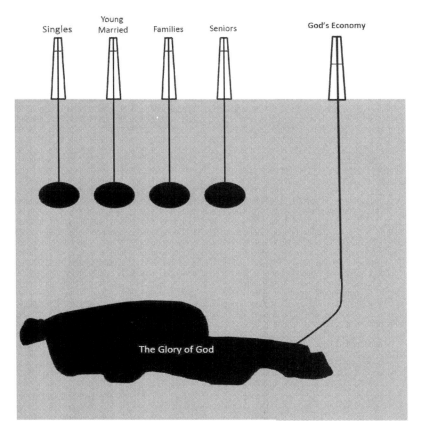

Singles Young Married Families Seniors God's Economy

The Glory of God

You have to cut across all the silos of life and go beyond looking to the Bible as answers to questions and ask yourself, "What's the point of the Bible?" The point of the Bible is that God made man to reflect his glory. Man sinned by setting himself up as his own god to steal glory from God and to be king on his own tiny throne. God's holiness demands that such rebellion merits eternal hell and judgment. But God's love is so overwhelming that he would send his own Son in the likeness of man to live a perfect life, satisfy all the requirements of God to be a perfect substitutionary sacrifice and take our place of condemnation on the cross. Through faith alone by grace alone in Christ alone we receive God's salvation. We live a renewed life for the glory of God. God brings us from death to life and offers us a new reality by which we partner with the Holy Spirit to bring about the gathering of the nations into one body, the Church, into this mystery. The Church advances the gospel to the ends of the earth bringing hope, healing, and reconciliation along the way. We continue this path until the consummation, where Christ returns, defeats all his enemies and establishes his kingdom. We, the

Church, rule over the entire universe with him, forever. All of this will result in praise to the glory of his name.

God in his gracious and loving way, establishes his dispensation, his economy to create a system of incentives and rewards to bring out the most innovation, creativity, and effort so that we are most fruitful in living for his glory. He will reward us all individually with recognition, reward, and responsibility in the next life. This life is a dress rehearsal for the next one.

If you drill deeper and cut across the silos that is what you would understand. What in that narrative speaks about finding your perfect job? What in that narrative is about living your best life now? What in that narrative is about going from success to significance? Nothing. Because the narrative of the Bible is not about you. It's not about me. Scripture is all about Christ. The Old Testament points toward Christ and the New Testament points back to Christ and our present life points toward our future with Christ. It's all Jesus, all the time.

The mother lode of going deeper in scripture is that you CAN live an incredibly joy filled, hope filled, passion filled life NOW as you join the Holy Spirit in this gathering of the nations. **That is your purpose**, whether you are a housewife, a CEO, a soldier, a teacher, a student, old, young, rich, poor. We are all part of this vine that is spreading out to the nations and gathering people who are red, yellow, black, and white into one people, the Church. And yes, there is some degree of searching, seeking, experimenting, discovering in finding a role that maximizes your gifting, but God has called us all to the gospel, to holiness, to bear fruit, and to be faithful, now.

This joy filled life always goes through trial and suffering. When we dig vertical wells of searching for answers in the Bible, we conveniently drill around verses that promise suffering, but when we start with the glory of God, suffering is always a part of the equation. But the mother lode of joy is knowing that God works all things for good and that he promises to repay all of the investment we make for his kingdom.

Go deeper. Cut across the silos to the mother lode in scripture, which is the glory of God.

The Word of God and Being Filled with the Spirit

I think people are confused about the Holy Spirit. Why is it that some supposedly "Spirit-filled" people spend too much time putting out fleeces (that means testing God circumstantially) and not enough time in the Word? In this section I would like to delve into what it means to be "in the Spirit."

> *You, however, are not in the flesh but in the Spirit, if in fact the Spirit of God dwells in you. Anyone who does not have the Spirit of Christ does not belong to him. Romans 8:9*

The word "in" is a very simple Greek Word "en." But this is the same "in" that Jesus uses when he says, "I am the vine; you are the branches. Whoever abides **in** me and I **in** him, he it is that bears much fruit, for apart from me you can do nothing" (John 15:5). Being filled with the Spirit is to be connected to the source of our strength, Jesus Christ himself. John goes on to say, "If you abide in me and **MY WORDS ABIDE IN YOU** [emphasis mine], ask whatever you wish, and it will be done for you" (John 15:7). This is why in Romans 8 the NIV translates "in" as "controlled by" because the sap of the vine controls the fruitfulness of the branches.

To be filled with the Spirit is to be filled with the words of the Spirit. This is not something that happens passively. We have to invest personally in hearing, reading, studying, memorizing, and meditating on the Word.[34] How is the Spirit supposed to fill and control you, if your mind is full of fleshly and worldly thoughts?

We also have to invest corporately in the Word. "Let the Word of Christ dwell in you richly, teaching and admonishing one another in all wisdom..." (Colossians 3:16). When the Bible is preached clearly and completely, the effect is godliness. "Him we proclaim, warning everyone and **teaching** everyone with all wisdom, that we may present everyone **mature** in Christ" (Colossians 1:28). The word "mature" *is teleion,* which means "perfect, complete, in fullness." When something reaches full consummation, achieving its intended aim, it is perfect.

This is why we need to elevate expository preaching in our pulpits. Expositional preaching of the Word of God is a means that the Holy Spirit uses to bring about spiritual maturity and perfection in the faith. Contrariwise, funny stories, skits, anecdotes, and motivational messages cannot bring about the *teleion* of the Spirit. How can we be filled with the

---

[34] Reference: the Navigators' "hand illustration."

Spirit, filled with his power, filled with his purpose, if we don't know his mind?

The mind of Christ does not come from looking for coincidence. The mind of Christ does not come from reading billboards for hidden messages. The mind of Christ does not come from reading into chance encounters. "You grew up in Kansas? I grew up in Kansas! We both live in NYC. God must have meant this to be!" There is so much confusion today about hearing God's voice, discerning God's Spirit, following the Spirit's lead, and the distinction is quite simple: If you're not in the Word, you're not listening to the Spirit. You may very well be listening to an entirely different spirit!

The King James Version says it best: "**Study** to shew thyself approved unto God, a workman that needeth not to be ashamed, **rightly dividing the Word of truth**" (2 Timothy 2:15). Study. Sit on your rear end. Open the book. Read. Memorize. Meditate. Study text. Study context. Look for themes, patterns, meta-narratives. Being filled with the Spirit can be hard work. All scripture is God-breathed – *theopneustos*. It is the very breath of God. The Spirit is the breath of God. How can you be filled with his breath? Inhale scripture. Study. Meditate.

Why do we need to study and meditate? To use a technology illustration: We need God to rewrite our hard drives. If you're not actively writing the Spirit's words onto your hard drive, the world and your flesh will fill that void. So much of our life is pure overflow so that when life squeezes us, what's inside comes out, and oh how ugly that may look! Inhaling scripture takes focus, not multi-tasking. The great lie of the 21st Century is that we can be more productive by multi-tasking. No! We work twice as long and are half as effective because we don't know how to focus on what is right in front of us.

The Spirit fills us, not with confusion from looking for signs, looking for coincidence, looking for happenstance. The Spirit fills us with the "knowledge of his will through all spiritual wisdom and understanding" (Colossians 1:9b). Paul goes on to pray, "May you be strengthened with all power, according to his glorious might, for all endurance and patience with joy" (Colossians 1:11). Knowledge, wisdom, understanding, power, might....these are the result of the Spirit's illuminating work. May you and I be filled with the Spirit today.

> *All scripture is given by inspiration of God, and is **profitable** for doctrine, for reproof, for correction, for instruction in righteousness.*
> *2 Timothy 3:16*

Priority #1: Grow in the Word

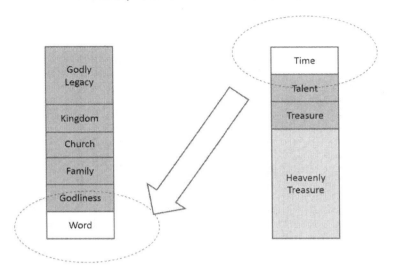

The grass withers, the flower fades, but the word of our God stands forever. Isaiah 40:8

Chapter 9 – ETERNAL ASSETS – Godliness
Producing the Fruit of Righteousness

Now may he who supplies seed to the sower, and bread for food, supply and multiply the seed you have sown and increase the fruits of your righteousness,
2 Corinthians 9:10

In God's economy, he blesses us with temporal resources to produce eternal assets. The balance sheet concept is a visualization to help us understand how it is possible to store up treasure (equity) in heaven. It's exciting to think that God designed a system, a dispensation, an economy where he, the owner, allows us, the managers, to steward his resources for the glory of his name. And the beauty of this system is that it produces the most innovation, the most creativity, the most productivity possible. This innovation is for one purpose, the glory of God in the exaltation of Christ as the gospel advances around the world. Ask yourself this: if we lived in a Communist country where there was no incentive for "gain" - everyone gets the same thing - wouldn't it follow that your own motivation to produce "fruit" or be productive would be greatly diminished? And that's exactly what we saw in the historical Soviet Union. No, the promise that all our labors get rewarded fuels us to strive further, faster, reach higher, dig deeper for Christ and his kingdom.

Fruit production is what we do EVERYDAY to transfer temporal resources and convert them into eternal assets. I want to help you think through how this happens every day:

- We move TOWARD godliness
- We move AWAY from sin

This is a daily challenge. By God's grace, we will produce fruit.

The challenge of the Christian life is that it is so "daily." God is evaluating our fruit, while kids are screaming, cars are honking, tempers are flaring. God is evaluating our fruit when there are work deadlines, stress levels are rising, nerves are fraying.... God is evaluating fruit, at all times, every day.

Being saved by grace does not give us license to minimize the importance of our everyday conduct. In God's economy, how we tip waitresses, how we interact with neighbors, how we demonstrate kindness and courtesy, how we curse when we're stuck in traffic, how we fret and complain, how we fill our time with mindless Internet surfing and texting...all of these are counted toward or against our eternal asset account. In God's economy, everything counts. Knowing this, we strive to be infectiously optimistic and inspirational examples in a dark and twisted world. We seek to grow the fruit of righteousness and Christ-likeness. And in doing so, we let our light shine so that all men might glorify our heavenly Father (Matthew 5:16).

Moving Toward Godliness

So, the first way that our resources move from the liability column (resources) to the asset column (fruit) is to think about "How do we spend our time?" And I would argue the most important decision you make every day is whether to abide in God's Word, or not. Simply overcoming the temptation to blow this off is a test. Is God first every day? You put God first, you dwell in his Word, you listen, and you meditate, and voila, fruit is produced.

I don't know how often I have to stress the importance of abiding in God's Word to produce fruit. Life is lived moment by moment. Believe it or not, thoughts think themselves. We are creatures of habit and go about our business without a lot of reflection on why we are making for ourselves a pot of coffee, why we are exercising on the treadmill, why we are showering, why we are going to work (or staying home), why we are shopping, why we get our hair cut, why we like to watch certain T.V. shows, why we eat dinner, and why we go to bed. We just do those things. And because most of our lives are not premeditated, as we interact with family, colleagues, passersby, we reveal our fruit.

God didn't give us a spouse and kids to make our lives miserable. God entrusted us with family to produce fruit, first your own, and then in the lives of your loved ones. So when they are getting on your nerves, which they do daily, God is giving you an opportunity to show what kind of fruit tree you are.

Without meditating on God's Word daily, I promise you, the fruit you will show will be ugly. Because life is lived in the moment, if the Word of God is not constantly in your thoughts, you will respond in ways that are not pleasing to the Lord. *"Thy Word have I hid in mine heart, that I might not sin against thee" (Psalm 119:11 KJV).*

So we move toward the daily disciplines of godliness. We pray. We study. I highly recommend a simple daily habit of putting God first in the first hour of the day. It sets the stage for the rest of the day. Personally, I get up, I hop on the elliptical and read the Bible. I don't watch T.V. while I exercise. As my body is moving I meditate on what I am reading and after 30 minutes I hop off and then I journal and pray. That first hour is so important, I cannot stress it enough.

While I drive to work I pray. I pray for family, I pray for colleagues, I pray over the day. I pray over every interaction that I imagine I will have that day and I ask God to make himself evident. As life presents different testing opportunities, the Word of God comes to mind and I am able to produce fruit by not reacting in the flesh. That Word will only come to mind if I've stored it up and if I've meditated on it.

If you're a stay at home mom like my wife is, I guarantee you, if you don't invest in the Word of God, you will spend your days reacting to your kids in the flesh. That's why that first hour is so important. For those that love to stay up in the wee-hours of night and sleep in, you'll have to adjust scripture devotions into your own life rhythm. But here's the rub: it would be foolish to think that your life will produce the fruit of godliness neglecting a consistent reading of the Word and prayer. Don't think you're better or smarter than the rest of us. No one lives a godly life on autopilot. The wise man listens to God's Word and puts it into practice (Matthew 7:24). Isn't that what Jesus said?

Meditating on the Word and applying it to our lives, every day, in every moment produces the fruit of the Holy Spirit. When we highly esteem God's holy name, the Holy Spirit gives us the power to live in an exemplary manner that accurately reflects his character and nature. Without saying a single word, people should be able to tell that we are Christian.

> *You are the light of the world. A city that is set on a hill cannot be hidden. Matthew 5:14*

> *But the fruit of the Spirit is love, joy, peace, longsuffering, kindness, goodness, faithfulness, gentleness, self-control. Galatians 5:22-23*

Living in a manner pleasing to the Lord is so vital to producing heavenly treasure. I have observed some people who think of kingdom building as simply developing, financing, and executing ministry projects. Their big egos get in the way and poison the waters of the organizations they are a part of. Rancor, strife, and resentment can pervade the cultures of ministries supposedly doing the work of the Lord.

Before we do stuff for God, we need to live in ways that reflect the beauty of his name.

How Meditating on the Word Produces the Fruit of Godliness

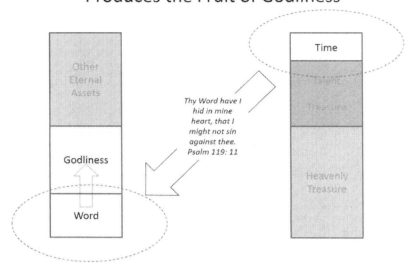

Move Away From Sin

There's one rule about sin. Run away! Don't flirt with sin. Don't mess with sin. Don't test temptation to see if you will get burned by its fire. Run away. The fruit of godliness begins with the Word of Christ richly dwelling in your heart. That fruit will cause you to revere Christ and revere his holy name. And that fruit will cause you to run from sin.

> *If your right eye causes you to sin, pluck it out and cast it from you; for it is more profitable for you that one of your members perish, than for your whole body to be cast into hell. And if your right hand causes you to sin, cut it off and cast it from you; for it is more profitable for you that one of your members perish, than for your whole body to be cast into hell. Matthew 5:29-30*

I'll be honest. For most of my life I haven't taken these verses seriously. Like the verses on heavenly treasure, I tended to view Jesus' words as pure metaphor, not pondering the gravity of sin.

If we truly honor God and value the glory of his name, we will not want anything to sully his reputation. Think of all the damage that has been done to the Church and Christ's kingdom because ministers, pastors, prominent Christians have fallen to scandal and moral failure. Don't the skeptics have a claim when they point out how much and how often Christ-followers commit adultery, how greedy we are, how unforgiving we are, how full of self-righteousness we are?

Like many men, I have struggled for years with lust. I tried all sorts of solutions with this tactic and that tactic. I experienced over and over some measure of victory but also continuing relapses of defeat. So, how did I break out of the cycle of sin? I got desperate in my soul. I imagined myself a moral failure and the damage I would do to Christ's reputation. So I cried out to God, "Lord, please kill me before I damage your reputation! Kill me. Cut me off. Please don't let me dishonor your name." Ever since then, I have experienced sustained victory from lustful thoughts like never before.

Practically that means some very simple things like not watching certain movies. Yeah, they might have some artistic value to them, but Christ's reputation is more important. Upholding our godliness should result in not surfing the Internet. I may need to do some fairly radical rearrangements to life in order to pull out all the weeds that might keep me from the fruit of righteousness. Christ's reputation is more important. Godliness demands constant vigilance, constant watchfulness, constant pruning. When do you get to relax from fighting sin? Never in this life.

And so we hope in the glory of God when we will be free from the power of sin and the very presence of sin. But until then, we fight. We fight a cunning enemy and we fight a flesh that will not quit, though it dwells in a grave. If you want fruit, you have to fight.

> For bodily exercise profiteth little: but **godliness** is **profitable** unto all things, having promise of the life that now is, and of that which is to come. 1 Timothy 4:8 KJV

Godliness is the fruit of spiritual disciplines.[35] Growing fruit in godliness comes from a renewed mind. We move toward holiness and sanctification by the Word of God and the power of the Spirit and away from sin. This is profitable because the fruit of godliness determines our assignment in the life to come.

---

[35] I recommend <u>Spiritual Disciplines for the Christian Life</u> by Donald S. Whitney and <u>The Pursuit of Holiness</u> by Jerry Bridges as more complete works on godliness.

Pure Religion

Pure and undefiled religion before God and the Father is this: to visit orphans and widows in their trouble, and to keep oneself unspotted from the world. James 1:27

Not only does godly character reflect the reality of the gospel in our lives, it creates capacity to be a world-changer. We glorify God by living pure and holy lives. But the purpose of godliness is not to create a Christian sub-culture, where we have as little contact with lost people as possible. In God's economy, living holy lives creates capacity to serve the least and the lost.

How does godliness create capacity? Right now so much of our capacity is filled with mindless clutter: tweeting, Facebook posting, selfie-taking, Pinterest pinning, T.V. watching, Internet surfing. While there is nothing wrong, per se, with any of those activities, on aggregate they completely consume our capacity. And in God's economy, time is the most important commodity. We can study and train ourselves harder to **sharpen our talent**. We can more wisely invest money to **increase our earthly treasure**. But there is **nothing we can do to get back wasted time**.

Godliness throws off all weights that hold us down from living all out for the gospel (Hebrews 12:1-2), even harmless fun. Why? Because we were meant for more. We were meant to use our capacity to help our neighbors, to serve the underprivileged, to love the unlovable. And when we waste our time on worthless idols, we squander the whole point of being godly, which is to be the hands and feet of Christ in a lost and dying world (James 1:27).

So when you find yourself completely consumed by the cares of the world and by constant screen time, when you find yourself unable to find time to pray, to love, to serve, ask yourself: Are these activities really making me more Christ-like? Am I using my capacity for the glory of God or am I wasting precious hours on worthless idols? At best, these time-consuming activities are a relaxing distraction. At worst, they infiltrate and pollute our hearts with covetousness (Proverbs 4:23).

Godliness produces fruit that is far greater and more important than creating a façade that we use to impress each other at church. At church we may look like we don't have problems, don't drink, smoke, curse, or hang out with "sinners." This can be fake godliness. The point of godliness is to reflect the awesome glory of God in our lives, to bring light into the darkness, and to join God in his work of redemption in the world (Ephesians 2:15-18).

Chapter 10 – ETERNAL ASSETS – Love
The Greatest Fruit is LOVE

The steadfast love of the Lord never ceases; his mercies never come to an end; they are new every morning; great is your faithfulness. Lamentations 3:22 – 23 ESV

In this is love, not that we loved God, but that He loved us and sent his Son to be the propitiation for our sins. 1 John 4:10

Since love is arguably the most important of all the fruit of the Holy Spirit, we need to take a step back and clarify the word "love." Net-net, we are receivers of love. In order for us to produce the fruit of love, to abound in love toward our family, our neighbors, our enemies, the world, we need that engine of love that only God can give to power us in this dark world.

God is faithful. Man is not. God establishes a covenant of love that man breaks. God upholds his part of the bargain. Man does not. God relentlessly reaches out his hand of mercy over thousands of years to the nation of Israel. Without the gospel and the Spirit, man cannot obey God's covenantal law. We have two thousand years of Jewish history to prove this. But "God so loved the world that he gave his only begotten son, that whosoever believes in him shall not perish, but have everlasting life" (John 3:16).

You read in 1 Kings, 2 Kings, 1 Chronicles, 2 Chronicles this pattern of God's love and faithfulness and man's idolatry. Over and over the people rebel against God and worship idols. Over and over God disciplines them through foreign conquerors. The people cry out. God remembers his covenant of love and relents his wrath. He saves. He blesses. The people prosper and then forget God. They worship false idols. Rinse, repeat story.

How many times would you try with your spouse, with your parents, with your family members before you gave up? What the Old Testament teaches us is that God's thousands of years of effort demonstrate that he is not an angry God as some portray him to be, but he is relentlessly loving. I enjoy reading the book of Hosea. Consider this:

> *I drew them with gentle cords, with bands of love, and I was to them*
> *as those who take the yoke from their neck. I stooped and fed them...*
> *My people are bent on backsliding from me.*
> *Though they call to the Most High,*

None at all exalt Him. Hosea 11:4, 7

So, after this pattern for hundreds and hundreds of years, would you forgive? We boil and stew over little transgressions and don't forgive. What kind of God would you be? Certainly not loving. But read further,

> *"How can I give you up, Ephraim?...*
> *My heart churns within me;*
> *My sympathy is stirred.*
>
> *"They shall walk after the Lord.*
> *He will roar like a lion.*
> *When He roars,*
> *Then his sons shall come trembling from the west;*
> *Hosea 11:8, 10*

We have the love of God backwards. When we think about God on a rescue mission, we view ourselves like innocent people trapped out at sea. The great hero sacrifices his life to save us. We, the good and noble people he saved, then remember his act of courage and live in honor of his name. That is not the gospel.

The gospel is that we are completely faithless to God and deserve only wrath. The nation of Israel is a mirror image of our faithlessness. Even on our best behavior we are constantly backsliding and constantly distracted by idols of Internet, work, sports, and movies, T.V., leisure, golf, almost anything and everything. The constant backsliding of the nation of Israel is a window into our souls. And no matter how hard we try, we fall short. Without his Spirit, we cannot please God.

Instead of giving us what we deserve, God gives his love and mercy. Does he do this because we are what we imagine ourselves to be, these beautiful but fallen creatures who just need a little bit of help? No, we are so utterly depraved that there is no good reason why God would or should love us, except this. He is love. "For I am God and not man" (Hosea 11:9). His love is so great that he finds a way in spite of his own holiness, which demands justice to our reckless rebellion. He takes the punishment we deserve, because his own character of love displayed for the world to see "when he roars" (Hosea 11:10) demonstrates his glory.

God demonstrates love because love displays his glory. And God's glory is above all things, most valuable to God. Do we really appreciate this love when we "pray the prayer" and then go off and live self-centered, depraved lives? Do we really know what love is? We don't.

Receiving his love means opening our eyes and with awe and wonder delighting in the awesomeness of his mighty deeds. Do we really do that in church world? Or do we recite John 3:16, pray the prayer, and then go about living lives that are mediocre, because we fear people's opinions? Does the love of God move our souls? Brokenness, joy, delight, gratitude should come crashing through our bitter hardened hearts as we contemplate the gospel and receive the love of God. God's love is so overwhelmingly powerful, so magnificently pure, so amazingly faithful, and so relentlessly wonderful. Is that what we think of his love? Does that move you? Does that move me?

And so, before we go off and show God how much we love him because "love is a verb," we need to pause and soak it in. His love is overwhelming. *In this is love, not that we loved God, but that He loved us and sent his Son to be the propitiation for our sins. 1 John 4:10*

Delighting in God's Love

Wondrously show your steadfast love, O Savior of those who seek refuge from their adversaries at your right hand. Keep me as the apple of your eye; hide me in the shadow of your wings. Psalm 17:7 – 8

The reason in the previous section why I focus on receiving the love of God is that we are extensions of his love to the world. We cannot give what we do not possess. And the reason why I focus on receiving God's love is that we are complete naïve fools to think that love exists apart from God. Human love is like water in a disposable cup, tiny, barely quenches a thirst, and empties itself with little gain. God's love is a never-ending ocean that springs up like a fountain in the heart of a believer who is known and loved by God.

> *If anyone thirsts, let him come to me and drink. He who believes in me, as the Scripture has said, out of his heart will flow rivers of living water." But this he spoke concerning the Spirit, whom those believing in him would receive... John 7:37b-39a*

We receive the Holy Spirit by faith in Jesus Christ. The Holy Spirit takes the Word of God and illuminates our hearts with it. We see with spiritual eyes the glory of God, where once we were enamored by everything but the glory of God. Seeing the glory of God in the gospel we respond with wonder, amazement, delight, gratitude. This produces fruit in our hearts that erupt in praise like lovers praise.

I love the Lord, because he has heard my voice and my supplications.
Because he has inclined his ear to me, therefore I will call upon Him
as long as I live. Psalm 116:1-2

Wondrously show your steadfast love, O Savior of those who seek
refuge from their adversaries at your right hand. Keep me as the
apple of your eye; hide me in the shadow of your wings.
Psalm 17:7-8

Do you see how King David writes? **He responds to God's salvation with
wonder and delight.** This element is missing in the Church today. We are
so mechanical toward God. I wonder if people love God or merely the idea
of loving God. I wonder if people love the God of the Bible or just love
knowledge of the Bible. What is missing from the Church are those heart
elements of awe, wonder, gratitude and delight. How can this be true? Test
yourself and see what you think about this verse:

You will show me the path of life;
In Your presence is fullness of joy;
At Your right hand are pleasures forevermore. Psalm 16:11

No. Let's be honest. Most American Christians are scared to get close to
God. Instead of believing that his presence brings fullness of joy, we believe
that if we get close to God he will send us to Africa, he will allow Satan to
attack, he will allow our kids to be hurt and so forth. Instead of running to
our heavenly Father, embracing him, rejoicing in his salvation, we opt for
the path of least resistance. Is that the love of lovers?

We are not rivers of living water, flowing with the love of God, bringing
hope and healing to the nations. We are stagnant pools with resources that
we've hoarded for ourselves on which we float about lazily, drink in hand.
In order for the Great Commission to be finished in our lifetime, it will take
all our time, talent, and treasure applied toward the glory of God. And the
engine of all of our efforts has to be love, not the mechanical version of love
we've concocted, but the love of lovers who would do anything to please the
Lord.

So what in our thinking needs to change? What needs to change is equating
doing things for God with love. Doing things for God is the result of love.
Believe it or not the action is not love itself. The doing is fruit.

If you love me, you will keep my commandments. John 14:15 ESV
Ean agapete me tas entolas tas emas teresete.
(Greek transliteration)

The word "ean" is a conditional word. "If this condition is true…" The word "teresete" is the future tense of "tereo," which means to hold, guard, and keep watch over. "Agapete" is the present subjunctive form of agape, meaning that the present act of loving God will result in keeping his commandments. We have mistranslated this verse in our popular Christian culture as "Love is a verb." Do love. Actually, we are to respond to God's love with wonder, delight, amazement, grief, and gratitude that results in our desire to do anything he asks us to do, and go anywhere he asks us to go.

The loving God piece is what's missing. We have substituted half-hearted acts of "love" that are primarily about justifying ourselves to ourselves. We often do the bare minimum to appear spiritual. The result is that we give 2% of our income and one or two hours per week worshiping and serving at church. The other 98% is used to indulge ourselves in the maddening chase to grow wealth and live the American Dream. Now I ask you, is that the love of God for God? Is that a demonstration of love for our fellow neighbor?

Loving Others

Greater love has no one than this, than to lay down one's life for his friends.
John 15:13
You shall love your neighbor as yourself. Matthew 22:39

If we truly understand and embrace the love of God, it will motivate us to love and serve others. This one is hard. Think of all the relationships that God puts in front of us. We are to love our wives as Christ loves the Church. We are to build up the Church and serve one another in love. We are to love those neighbors we barely know the way the Good Samaritan loved his fellow neighbor. It's an exhausting thought. If I'm loving and serving so many people, when do I get downtime? Do I ever get a break? And so we water down the definition of love into something that looks like tolerance. We tolerate each other as long as they don't mess with our stuff and ruin our property values. But if the kingdom of God is to advance to the ends of the earth, it will take an enormous amount of love, compelled by the love of Christ himself.

Jesus says, "If you love me, you will keep my commandments." The first part is the root. The second part is the fruit.[36] If we love God…if we feel

---

[36] The idea that love is the root and obedience is the fruit has come directly from many, many John Piper sermons I have listened to.

high esteem, affection, and delight in God then we will obey his commandments. And what is that commandment? His commandment is that we love one another (John 13:34). If we don't esteem God, find delight in Christ our Savior, then our "love" looks a lot like dutiful drudgery.

Loving people is a spillover from the love of God filling our hearts based on the gratitude we have to Christ for the cross. And the result of that is loving others by serving them.

> So when he had washed their feet, taken his garments, and sat down again, he said to them, "Do you know what I have done to you? You call me Teacher and Lord, and you say well, for so I am. **If I then, your Lord and Teacher, have washed your feet, you also ought to wash one another's feet.** For I have given you an example, that you should do as I have done to you. Most assuredly, I say to you, a servant is not greater than his master; nor is he who is sent greater than he who sent him. If you know these things, blessed are you if you do them. John 13:12-17

The greatest fruit in your eternal asset column is love. All of the eternal assets must be motivated by love. In fact, Paul goes so far as to say that without love, all the rest is worthless. With the eternal balance sheet, maybe the phrase "without love, it profits me nothing" (1 Corinthians 13:3) makes more sense. We can go through the motions, making love a verb and dutifully doing things for God, like we're doing him a favor. Or, we can out of deep gratitude and high esteem for his name, respond to the gospel and love others. We can serve them even though our flesh might feel that washing feet is a humiliating exercise. Why? Because our reward in heaven will be great.

> But if you love those who love you, what credit is that to you? For even sinners love those who love them. And if you do good to those who do good to you, what credit is that to you? For even sinners do the same. And if you lend to those from whom you hope to receive back, what credit is that to you? For even sinners lend to sinners to receive as much back. **But love your enemies, do good, and lend, hoping for nothing in return; and your reward will be great.** Luke 6:32-35a

The Importance of Love

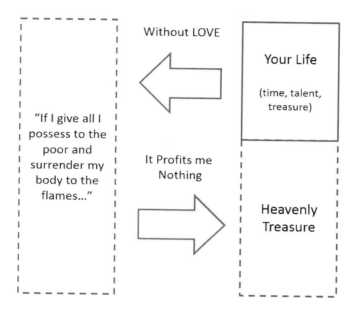

In God's economy loving others is the fruit that demonstrates the reality of the gospel. We love because he first loved us. We joyfully serve one another without human applause knowing that our heavenly Father will reward us in heaven.

> *And if I give all my possessions to feed the poor, and if I surrender my body to be burned, but **do not have love, it profits** me nothing.*
> *1 Corinthians 13:3 NASB*

On the eternal balance sheet, you can either think of love as part of your godliness account or love surrounding the entire asset column. I called it out separately because love is that important. May we all, by the power of the Holy Spirit, love one another as Christ loved us.

> *Dear children, let us not love with words or speech but with actions and in truth. 1 John 3:18 NIV*

> *Give thanks to the Lord for he is good. His love endures forever. Psalm 107:1*

Chapter 11 – ETERNAL ASSETS – Reproduction

Seeking Lost People and Reproducing Spiritual Children

Be fruitful and multiply. Genesis 1:28

Spiritual Reproduction

When God gives Adam and Eve the command to be fruitful and multiply, he was explaining one of the most basic concepts of glory. God's glory is seen most fully in the image of the Son. He is reproducing that image over and over by regenerating human hearts and by bringing them to full maturity. We participate in extending his glory to the ends of the earth by reproducing his image through evangelism and discipleship, in our physical children and in our spiritual children.

In God's economy, seeking and saving the lost accrue massive gains in the eternal asset column. The reason is simple: the human soul lives forever. Christ's example in seeking, pursuing, and redeeming the lost should motivate us to go all out for the sake of the gospel. Evangelism is hard work, but the joy set before us is worth it.

Observe yourself when it comes to golf, if you're an avid enthusiast. Do you give up because it's difficult? Does the fact that a certain course kicked your rear cause you to throw in the towel and say, "That's the last time I'll ever play that game. Golf is so futile." No. Golf enthusiasts double-down, triple-down, and practice, practice, practice in the midst of setbacks and failures. Why? They do it to win the prize of self-satisfaction. There is a component of joy in the hope that one day all the stars will align and they will score an "eagle" or even a hole-in-one.

If we go back to eternal assets, what is the overarching theme of what is eternal? The mega-theme of scripture is the glory of God. Glory is the many attributes of God that can be seen and apprehended with the senses. We love and long for glory. When everything comes together, hard work, perfection, beauty, and drama we experience glory. When your son or daughter perfectly performs at a recital or at a sporting event, we lean in and we experience joy. When your favorite sports team wins right before the buzzer, you lean in and experience joy. When you swing your golf club and make a perfect drive, you lean in and experience joy. GLORY. And what we see in this life is that we are endlessly motivated by our own glory.

Winning lost souls is for the glory of God. Living the gospel every day means reenacting the drama of Christ's sacrificial love to redeem for himself a people out of darkness, illuminating their minds to transform enemies of God into citizens of another kingdom. If we could see with spiritual eyes the amazing drama, the spiritual warfare, the colossal power of the cross, we would lean in. We would rejoice at every lost sinner that converts.

So in Luke Chapter 15, Jesus gives three parables in succession about the lost: the lost sheep, the lost coin, and the lost (prodigal) son. And what you learn from these parables is that the currency, that true wealth that we are going to receive in heaven, is joy. Joy is the currency of heaven. Joy is the reward for investing in that which is eternal. And in three successive parables Jesus tells us that lost people matter to our heavenly Father.

> *What man of you, having a hundred sheep, if he loses one of them, does not leave the ninety-nine in the wilderness, and go after the one which is lost until he finds it? And when he has found it, he lays it on his shoulders, rejoicing. And when he comes home, he calls together his friends and neighbors, saying to them, 'Rejoice with me, for I have found my sheep which was lost!' I say to you that likewise **there will be more joy in heaven** over one sinner who repents than over ninety-nine just persons who need no repentance. Luke 15: 4-6*

We get so comfortable in our churches. We want the seating to feel comfortable. We want the coffee to taste good. We want the air conditioning to be just right. We want the music to fit our personal tastes. We want the sermon to be short, sweet, and just speak to our relevant needs. That's it. That's what most of us contemplate concerning our religious lives. It's about us. And yet the parable of the lost sheep speaks of Jesus' heart. His heart is out there with drunkards, prostitutes, orphans, widows, tax collectors.

What I see is intentionality. I see a picture of a shepherd, with scuffed up knees and knuckles, reaching out to a lost sheep on a craggy cliff. There is someone out there that God has laid on your heart, a neighbor, a co-worker, a family member. If we follow Christ's model, we would pursue that lost soul with relentless love.

But perhaps you've already given up on him. Maybe you've already said, "He won't change, or she won't change." Are you leaning in to the gospel? What credit is that to you if you give up? What credit is that to your heavenly treasure?

We see in Luke 15 three times a picture of our shepherd, Jesus Christ as pressing in, leaning in, sacrificing himself to save lost souls. Why? For the joy set before him, the Son endures hardship, suffering, and pain. Joy. He is looking forward to the consummation of the mystery of the marriage of Christ and the Church. Unless you have spiritual eyes, unless you have the love of God, this drama means nothing. You may be more motivated to go golfing than joining in the greatest drama in the history of the universe, the gospel of the glory of God. History is indeed his story.

Our part of his story is to seek and save the lost. Look at the second parable. This one is strange.

> Or what woman, having ten silver coins, if she loses one coin, does not light a lamp, sweep the house, and search carefully until she finds it? And when she has found it, she calls her friends and neighbors together, saying, 'Rejoice with me, for I have found the piece which I lost!' Likewise, I say to you, there is joy in the presence of the angels of God over one sinner who repents. Luke 15:8-10

This woman calls her friends to have a party over finding a lost coin. Now because we don't use coins that much in America, we think, "No big deal! She found a quarter." No, the silver coins were her life's wealth, her accumulated wages. Each coin represented a significant portion of her total net worth. A coin may seem like a trivial amount to you, but in the context of billions of people living on less than two dollars per day, perhaps you can appreciate the value of one silver coin. Do you see the connection now with your heavenly treasure and lost souls? She doesn't wax poetically about predestination. She overturns the furniture looking for the lost coin. Seeking the lost is an active process. Trusting in God's sovereignty is not incompatible with the effort required to bring souls to Christ.

And then finally, the most beautiful story of the three is the story of the lost son or most commonly, "The Story of Prodigal Son." The Prodigal Son demands his inheritance early. He then wastes his money on prostitutes, gambling, and partying. He snaps back to his senses and begins the long journey home to ask his father's forgiveness.

> But when he was still a great way off, his father saw him and had compassion, and ran and fell on his neck and kissed him. And the son said to him, 'Father, I have sinned against heaven and in your sight, and am no longer worthy to be called your son.'
> "But the father said to his servants, 'Bring out the best robe and put it on him, and put a ring on his hand and sandals on his feet. And bring the fatted calf here and kill it, and let us eat and be merry; for

this my son was dead and is alive again; he was lost and is found.'
And they began to be merry. Luke 15: 20-24

A patriarch in those days would never run. He was too dignified. And yet, every day as he waited, we see a picture of the father scanning the horizon, leaning in, looking for his son. When he sees him, he sprints. This picture of God running is so foreign to all of us who grew up in the church and "prayed the prayer" to receive Christ at age 5. You see, many of us don't think of ourselves as lost. We think, "I've always known Jesus. I've always loved Jesus." We don't resonate with Paul's words,

> *All of us also lived among them at one time, gratifying the desires of the sinful nature. Like the rest, we were by nature, objects of wrath. Ephesians 2: 2-3 NIV*

It takes faith to believe this passage, especially if you were raised in the church. If you don't feel the weight of your sin and the price that Christ paid to redeem you then the thought of him running feels completely foreign. *Why does he need to run? I prayed the prayer.* That's why the majority of church membership testimonies I read say something like, "I believed but I didn't walk with Christ until after college, when everything in my life crumbled around me. Then I realized I needed God..."

Sometimes God allows us in his almighty providence to wander, just like the lost son, in order to jolt us to our senses. And then we humbly come to the cross for forgiveness.

If we realized the colossal magnitude of the cross, of what it meant for Christ to forgive us, shouldn't we want that for others? Shouldn't we want that for our Somali, Cambodian, Vietnamese, Hmong, Black, White, Red neighbors? Why is it in church world we are so oblivious to lost people? Why do we care so much about feeling comfortable at church? It's because we don't feel the weight of our sin and the amount of sacrifice it took to save us.

If we just knew what a big deal this was in the cosmic scheme of things, if we understood that God's entire economy is designed to seek and save lost people, we'd be motivated to complete the Great Commission. There are seven BILLION people on this planet. In God's economy, he cares about lost sinners. Just read the story of Jonah. As for predestination, let God be God. In his providence he has chosen some to destruction, but what is that to us (Romans 9:22)? We are to seek and save that which is lost (Luke 19:10). That is our role in God's economy.

What will it take for us to go the extra mile? We would go the extra mile if our own equity were on the line. Like the lost coin we would seek the treasure of seeing the joy of the Lord in a repentant sinner, so much so, that we would overturn every bit of furniture to find. Lean in to the glory of God. Heaven waits with bated breath for every repentant sinner to call on the name of the Lord.

ASSETS

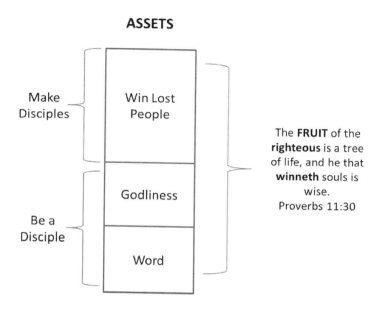

For God so loved the world that he gave his only begotten son, that whosoever believeth in him should not perish, but have everlasting life. John 3:16 (KJV)

And this is eternal life, that they may know you, the only true God, and Jesus Christ whom you have sent. John 17:3

Chapter 12 – ETERNAL ASSETS – Regeneration
The Necessity of the Holy Spirit's Work

Not by might, nor by power, but by my Spirit, saith the Lord. Zechariah 4:6b

One of the main problems with modern evangelicalism and how we communicate the gospel is that we emphasize our responsibility, to a fault. Like good Americans, we want people to take responsibility for their actions. Own up, fess up, man up, step up. Everything is about us, even salvation. Decide, decide, decide. We obsess about decisions and how many decisions were made, and how many people came forward. We've not only taken the mystery out of salvation, we've taken the Holy Spirit out of salvation.

In John's famous narrative of Nicodemus, we see a venerable Pharisee visit Christ at night. He asks Jesus about the kingdom and Jesus replies,

> *Unless one is born again, he cannot see the kingdom of God...Truly, truly, I say to you, unless one is born of water and the Spirit, he cannot enter the kingdom of God. That which is born of the flesh is flesh, and that which is born of the Spirit is spirit. Do not marvel that I said to you, 'You must be born again.' The wind blows where it wishes, and you hear its sound, but you do not know where it comes from or where it goes. So it is with everyone who is born of the Spirit." John 3:3, 5-8*

When Nicodemus protests, Jesus says, *"Are you not the teacher of Israel and yet you do not understand these things" (John 3:10)?* It may be that Jesus was referring to Ezekiel 37, the vision of the Valley of Dry Bones.

> *And he led me around among them, and behold, there were very many on the surface of the valley, and behold, they were very dry. And he said to me, "Son of man, can these bones live?" And I answered, "O Lord God, you know." Then he said to me, "Prophesy over these bones, and say to them, O dry bones, hear the Word of the LORD. Thus says the LORD God to these bones: Behold, I will cause breath to enter you, and you shall live. Ezekiel 37:2-5*

After Ezekiel prophesies, the dry bones become inanimate flesh and blood.

> *Then he said to me, "Prophesy to the breath; prophesy, son of man, and say to the breath, thus says the LORD God; Come from the four winds, O breath, and breathe on these slain, that they may live. Ezekiel 37:9-10*

What both Ezekiel and John's narrative describe is the work of regeneration. That is, God grants salvation by the Holy Spirit breathing life into dead hearts and dead bodies. The Bible clearly states that we are dead in our sins. Dead means dead. And other than Jesus, dead men do not resurrect themselves.

This is the essence of the problem with how we frame salvation. We ask people to pray a prayer like it's an incantation. Substantively, we are no different than pagans in this regard. The incantation forces the deity to bring rain, cause crops to grow, etc., etc. But Jesus declares, *"The wind blows where it wishes."* In other words, God is sovereign. We can no more decide our own salvation than we can capture the wind. In fact, people who quote John 1:12 often forget to quote John 1:13 to get a more complete picture of salvation.

> *But to all who did receive him, who believed in his name, he gave the right to become children of God, who were born, not of blood nor of the will of the flesh, nor of the will of man, but of God. John 1:12-13*

You and I don't will ourselves to salvation by making the veins in our head pop while we pray the Sinner's Prayer. If I get really emotional, or say to myself, "I'm being very earnest" while I pray the prayer, none of those necessitates salvation.

What Ezekiel describes is this: God sovereignly does the work of salvation through his Holy Spirit. But he allows his saints to participate in that work through the preaching of the Word of God. *"Faith comes from hearing the message, and the message through the Word of God" (Romans 10:26).* In other words, God can use any means he wants in his sovereignty to save sinners. That is his divine prerogative. But, he declares in scripture that the mechanism he uses most is Spirit-filled preaching of the Word. Something special happens when we join with Christ by accurately and powerfully presenting the gospel. God in his sovereignty, [sometimes, many times] will send his Spirit to bring conviction to the human soul. That conviction is a response to the preaching of the Word and like the rattling of the bones and the bringing of the sinews and the flesh together, you can often see the effect that the gospel has on people. But what the Ezekiel passage teaches is that the final, decisive work of salvation belongs to God alone. The preaching does its work but there is no life. The Holy Spirit does his work and regeneration comes. Faith comes. And as the regenerated heart starts to beat, the first gasp of air from the regenerated person, in response to the gospel is "I believe!"

What John 3 and Ezekiel 37 should teach us, practically, are the following: One, what saves people are not celebrity Christians. I love hearing their testimonies. And indeed, their testimonies are powerful. But what has started to pervade the evangelical world is a loss of faith in the powerful preaching of the Word and an overdependence on creating "relevant events." We subconsciously believe that it is Mr. Celebrity Christian's testimony that saves, not Christ through his Word. And by degrading the sufficiency of scripture, we also degrade the importance of simply, accurately, and powerfully proclaiming the message. Why do we equate the Spirit's work to getting people to some emotional state after listening to a moving testimony, turning down the lights, and playing soft music? That is not how salvation occurs. And if we actually believed that we are responsible for delivering the message and God is responsible for saving, we might actually share the gospel more.

What we've created in our churches is this fake pressure to get people to raise their hands and pray a prayer. People think, "I'm not gifted to get people to respond. I can't do that. Maybe Billy Graham can, but I can't." Believe it or not, Billy can't either! But, we've created a whole system of evangelistic events that emphasizes celebrity speakers that neglects the real power, the Holy Spirit himself. And like Ezekiel, our prayers to the Holy Spirit should be like Jacob wrestling with the angel. We should be pleading with God to move in human hearts. We should so forcefully pray to God to bring salvation that it looks like Ezekiel prophesying to the breath. Observe Ezekiel commanding the breath. "Come from the four winds and breathe!" Jacob wrestling sounds like, "I will not let you go until you bless me" (Genesis 32:26)! Praying for our unsaved husband, wife, son, daughter, brother, sister, friend looks like, "God, you have to move. You alone can rescue. You alone can save. So by your Spirit **change their hearts of stone into hearts of flesh!**"

> *Salvation belongs to our God who sits on the throne, and to the*
> *Lamb...   Amen! Blessing and glory and wisdom,*
> *Thanksgiving and honor and power and might,*
> *Be to our God forever and ever.*
> *Amen." Revelation 7:10, 12*

In God's economy seeking and saving that which was lost is worth 100x more fruit than sitting around in our holy huddles "fellowshipping." Jesus gives three parables to emphasize the heart of our Father: Heaven's hosts rejoice *more* when lost sinners repent. They will welcome you into eternal dwellings when this life ends. When we grow in the fruit of the Word, grow in the fruit of the Holy Spirit, we will naturally (supernaturally) take the seed that the fruit produces and plant it in others. That seed will, by the power of the Holy Spirit, bear fruit in others. All of that fruit accrues to our account and heavenly treasure.

> For **what is a man profited**, if he shall gain the whole world, and **lose his own soul**? *Matthew 16:26a KJV*

> 'Not by might nor by power, but by My Spirit,' says the Lord of hosts. *Zechariah 4:6b*

Chapter 13 – ETERNAL ASSETS – Discipleship

Go therefore and make disciples of all nations, baptizing them in the name of the Father and of the Son and of the Holy Spirit, teaching them to observe all that I have commanded you. And behold, I am with you always, to the end of the age. Matthew 28:19-20 ESV

We should not divorce evangelism from discipleship, as if they are two different paths. They are not. The Great Commission does not ask us to go and have people recite the Sinner's Prayer. The passage says, *"teaching them to observe all things that I have commanded you" (Matthew 28:20a).* In other words, sharing the gospel is just the beginning.

The reason why clearly articulating the gospel is just the beginning is that we don't know what kind of soil the Word of God lands on. We don't know if an indication of faith is the same as saving faith. Sometimes it is. Sometimes it is not. The fruit depends on what kind of soil the Word falls on.

> *Behold, a sower went out to sow. And as he sowed, some seed fell by the wayside; and the birds came and devoured them. Some fell on stony places, where they did not have much earth; and they immediately sprang up because they had no depth of earth. But when the sun was up they were scorched, and because they had no root they withered away. And some fell among thorns, and the thorns sprang up and choked them. But others fell on good ground and yielded a crop: some a hundredfold, some sixty, some thirty. Matthew 14: 3-8*

Our goal in presenting the gospel to our own children and to our friends is to shepherd them through the entire process of hearing the Word, receiving the Word, and growing in the Word unto fruitfulness. Yes, there may be times when you share the gospel with complete strangers, but the vast majority of the time you will know the person. Their fruit accrues to your account! So why would any of us want someone to "pray the prayer" and not demonstrate any fruit?

> *I have planted, Apollos watered; but God gave the increase. 1 Corinthians 3:6*

We are not responsible for the fruit. We focus on what is in our span of control, which is setting the conditions for fruitfulness. **We are responsible for seed and soil.** A good farmer tills the soil, plants seed, fertilizes the ground, pulls out weeds, sprays for bugs, and waters the young shoots. A good farmer knows that there is a lot completely out of her control. But she focuses on what is in her control knowing that on balance, her field will be full of good crop.

Discipleship and growing in fruitfulness is a team event. That is why God gave us the Church. But let me be clear: it is FRUIT that accrues to our account, not decisions. What I observe in some large evangelistic events, crusades, and missions trips is a lot of cheering about decisions for Christ, and a lack of commensurate follow through. If no one takes responsibility for discipleship, how can we expect there to be any fruit? If you care about your heavenly reward, you will care about the maturity of your spiritual offspring. Fruitfulness is maturity.

Winning souls to Christ is major fruit! Growing those souls to maturity in Christ is even more fruit. And spiritually mature people evangelize. The disciples of your disciples are even more fruit credited to your account. If you are not discipling people to be people who win and disciple others, your fruit gets cut short.

People constantly wrestle with the supposed distinction between evangelism and discipleship. I think about Amazon.com and how they care about every single transaction that occurs. Their response to a single dissatisfied customer is legendary and yet we all know that Amazon is not content at winning just one customer. They want loyalty (fruit) AND exponential growth (multiplication). There is no tradeoff between discipleship and evangelism. If we actually believed that everything counts toward our heavenly equity, we would exhibit similar, dare I say fanatical, care and feeding of disciples, as well as tenacious pursuit of lost people.

> I have chosen you, and ordained you, that ye should go and bring
> forth fruit, and that your fruit should remain... John 15:16 KJV

In the Parable of the Sower, Jesus commends bearing much fruit, 100x to be exact. What credit is it to our account if the fruit does not endure? What credit is it to our account if our "converts" raise their hands and subsequently show no fruit in keeping with repentance? If we care about our heavenly equity, we'd press in and ensure the conditions for fruitfulness. Hence, discipleship and evangelism go hand in hand.

Discipling Your Family

Blessed is the man who fears the Lord, who delights greatly in his commandments. His descendants will be mighty on the earth; the generation of the upright will be blessed. Psalm 112: 1-2

Most likely the majority of your time, talent, and treasure will be spent on growing fruitfulness in your family. I will address specifically what parents should do in Chapters 18 and 19.

God cares about his own glory. His glory is best seen in the face of Christ. The gospel is the delivery vehicle by which his glory multiplies from sea to shining sea in the hearts of believers. In the Church we can all participate in growth whether in planting, water, fertilizing, cultivating, or harvesting. During the course of our walk in Christ, in the Church, we will disciple our own kids, other people's children, and disciples at every stage of spiritual maturity. Our contribution toward their growth and maturity is credited to our heavenly treasure! And what Luke 15 tells me in three successive parables is this: God cares about lost people, shouldn't we?

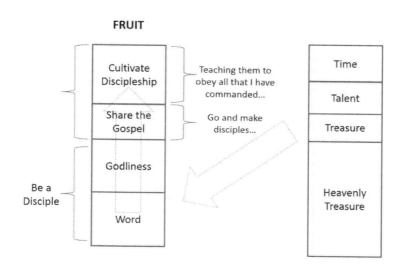

And the things that you have heard from me among many witnesses, commit these to faithful men who will be able to teach others also. 2 Timothy 2:2

Chapter 14 – ETERNAL ASSETS – The Church

Love the Bride of Christ

"Lord, do not trouble yourself, for I am not worthy to have you come under my roof. Therefore I did not presume to come to you. But say the word, and let my servant be healed. For I too am a man set under authority, with soldiers under me: and I say to one, 'Go,' and he goes; and to another, 'Come,' and he comes; and to my servant, 'Do this,' and he does it." When Jesus heard these things, he marveled at him, and turning to the crowd that followed him, said, "I tell you, not even in Israel have I found such faith." Luke 7:6-9

It's easy to be down on the church. The institutional church, whether that be your denomination or the formal organization of your local church can seem clueless at times. I confess I sometimes look down on church people. I confess I've been guilty of saying, "the church doesn't get it" too many times. For many years I was enamored with para-church organizations unencumbered by church structures and church politics. They could act faster and more decisively than the church.

Believing that God's kingdom will advance primarily and decisively outside of the Church is an indicator of poor theology and a lack of faith. Do you believe Jesus' words, *"Upon this rock I will build my church and the gates of hell will not prevail against it"* (Matthew 16:18)? Do you believe that the Church is Christ's bride and that the Church will rule with him for eternity? If you believe God's Word then you need to love the Church. You need to love the Church in general and your local church in particular. God's plan to redeem the world is through the Church and there is no plan B.

What is amazing is how the Roman centurion in Luke 7 describes himself as a man under authority. He understands that God works through authority, even ungodly people who are in authority. By being under authority, by submitting to spiritual authority in a local church, what you are saying is the following: "I'm not the smartest person. I don't have all the answers." When we think or talk negatively about the church aren't we really puffing ourselves up, as if our ways are higher than God's ways? Aren't we really elevating ourselves when we constantly put church leadership down?

To be under authority is really a sign of humility. Just like Christ humbled himself and became a servant, so too, we should humble ourselves and in our local church be the servant of all. When we serve in our local church, we are in essence agreeing with Christ and saying, "Amen. Your ways are perfect and you WILL advance your kingdom through your Bride."

What does that look like? I think it looks like membership. "What? David, isn't membership a man-made thing?" To some extent, that is true. But as a test of faith, you are planting your flag in a local, Bible-teaching church. And just like Christ demonstrates his fidelity to his Bride, so we too demonstrate our fidelity to Christ's Bride by not jumping around from church to church based on things like music, children's programming, the food, even the quality of the preaching.

"What? David, the quality of preaching is the most important thing I'm looking for!" I'm going to say something others will disagree with. **Preaching is not the most important trait to look for in a church.** When my wife and I moved to the suburbs of Minneapolis, we didn't rush to Bethlehem Baptist just to hear John Piper. My wife and I planted our flag at the first Bible-believing church we visited. This church did indeed have a strong preacher, but what was important was to plant our flag, to be under authority, and to grow in a local, Bible-believing community of faith.

People who know what church I go to might protest that we have one of the best preachers in the country. That is true, but I practiced this discipline while I was in the Army. For nine years I went to the local military chapel. That was my community of faith, period. Some chaplains preached better than others. But you see, the Bible doesn't tell us to keep moving around looking for the best preaching. The Bible says,

> Let us not forsake the assembling of ourselves, as is the habit of some, but let us encourage one another, all the more, as you see the day approaching. Hebrews 10:26

If you think church is about being entertained and getting your itches scratched through good music and good preaching, be prepared to be on the road constantly. You might never be satisfied. If you don't settle down in a local church, don't expect to see fruit in your life.

You see going to church is not like going to a Toastmasters event. You're not coming to hear the best speakers. It's more like the battalion aid station behind the front lines. You temporarily leave the front lines of war to get patched up, to receive encouragement, to encourage others, and then on Monday to head back to the front lines again. We are in a spiritual war. We don't always get to choose who is next to us in our foxhole. Hopping from church to church looking for entertainment shows we are on vacation, not engaged in a spiritual war.

What weary soldiers need is to worship corporately. The battle of life can feel lonely. I've talked to so many people who work in Corporate America who feel completely isolated in their faith from Monday through Friday. We need to worship because when we corporately declare the worthiness of Christ, our minds snap back from self-pity and self-focus to God-focus. We are on this earth to make Christ famous. We worship simply because God deserves our honor and praise.

How utterly silly it is to turn this around and think that Sunday worship is about me? So what if the preaching isn't the best? Doesn't God still deserve our time? Doesn't God deserve our heart-felt praise even if the praise band isn't the best? Aren't we demonstrating narcissism when we get upset at the selection of praise music? The Bible says we are to worship God in the splendor of his holiness (Psalm 96:9). His splendor is an objective reality, not a subjective experience based on how good the music or the sermon was.

So, what do you do if the music isn't good and the preaching isn't up to your standards? One, pray for the worship leader and pastor. I mean it. Bless them in your prayers and in your thinking. Encourage them. Say nice things about them. Refuse to get caught up in gossiping (sin) or complaining (also sin) about the music or the preaching. Remind your fellow church goers, "Worship is not about us, it's about the worthiness of Christ." I tell you, even if the music and the preaching don't get objectively better, you will be blessed. God will bless you because you are being a blessing. And that's the point of the Christian life, isn't it? Sunday worship is not about going to church to get your funny bone scratched. Worship fuels our hearts to be a blessing to the nations.

Well, what if my church strays toward liberal theology and rejects the supremacy of scripture? What if my pastor starts preaching false doctrine? If either are true, **just get up and leave**. Don't sit under false teaching. God will judge those who lead his children astray very harshly (Luke 17:2). I wouldn't want to be in the impact zone.

But let's be honest. Most of the time, this is not the case. Most of us go to a perfectly good, Bible-believing church. The problem is you. You bring yourself with your sin, your neediness, your emotional baggage with you to church. There is no perfect church. But that's fine. The blessing is that we all are sinners and have fallen short of the glory of God. We are all saved by his amazing grace. And that's what we extend to one another, grace. So pray for your pastor. Serve your local church with zest and enthusiasm. You will be blessed and you will be fruitful. I promise you.

You know, there was a time when I was getting so fed up with church world that I was in danger of letting the root of bitterness poison my worship of God. You know what God did? He had the senior pastor of my local church approach me to be an elder. What, me an elder? That blindsided me. The elder application form asks if you've been called to be an elder. I honestly wrote that I didn't know if I was called specifically for this, but I was open to whatever God had for me. I was confirmed by church vote and then joined the board of elders.

Then the most amazing thing happened. I fell in love with the Church. I can't fully explain it. Acting as a shepherd of Christ's flock, the Lord gave me a heart to love his sheep, his people. I couldn't be an elder without loving his church. So, I started to pray for the church, for specific people, for pastors, for other elders. Often in the middle of the hallway, my wife and I would close a conversation by praying with fellow worshipers.

Some people asked me if I felt like there was a bulls-eye on my back when I responded to the call to become an elder. This is the church equivalent of saying, "Don't lift your head up too much or it might get chopped off." As I think back I can see that trials continued to grow, but overall my tenure as an elder has been a joy filled blessing. I've had the privilege of getting to know other pastors and elders, men I truly admire and respect. Any of the elders could legitimately say to me, "Follow me as I follow Christ" and I could learn a great deal from each and every one of them. My wife and I have been overwhelmingly blessed at our local church, even as we have sought to be a blessing to others.

So, I urge you. Join your local church. Quit dating the church and acting like you're smarter than everyone else. You're not smarter than King Jesus. He promised that the Church would storm the very gates of hell. Do you believe that's true? Then grow in faithfulness to your local church. If the preaching isn't everything you want it to be there are plenty of streaming sermons online. But the real fruit will come when you join your local church and grow in your sanctification by being a blessing. Serve. Love. Give. Your fruit will grow and God will channel his blessings through you.

> **Obey your leaders** and submit to them, for they keep watch over your souls as those who will give an account. Let them do this **with joy** and **not with grief, for this would be** unprofitable for you.
> Hebrews 13:17

Use Your Spiritual Gifts

...to equip the saints for the work of ministry, for building up the body of Christ, until we all attain to the unity of the faith and of the knowledge of the Son of God, to mature manhood, to the measure of the stature of the fullness of Christ... Ephesians 4:12-13

Once you are under authority, planting your flag in a local Bible-believing church, it's time to serve. Growing in faith is a team sport. You will cut your fruit short if you think you can sit at home and watch television sermons and not serve as an active member of a local congregation. In God's economy, spiritual gifts are in the liability column. They are temporal and do not endure for eternity, but are essential to producing fruit. My emphasis in this section is where spiritual gifts fit in God's economy; [I will not address all the voluminous and controversial issues surrounding the gifts.]

In Chapter 17, I go into greater detail about the process in which the liability (resource) column grows. Maximizing and monetizing human capital is a large component of this. Spiritual gifts, too are a resource for growing eternal assets but they function differently. Instead of human capital converting into financial capital before transferring over the asset column, spiritual gifts are deployed directly from the liability column into the Church. When we don't use our spiritual gifts to serve the Church, we are in fact robbing the Church of her resources. There is no such thing as a Lone Ranger Christian.

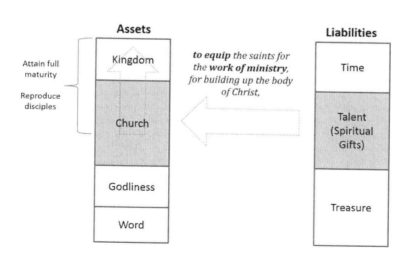

The Church is not only the means of advancing the gospel, but the Church is the prize. Not only is God our inheritance (Psalm 16:5), but we are his inheritance (Psalm 94:14)! Therefore, in God's economy, we are preparing for Jesus Christ to receive his inheritance, his Bride! In Ephesians 5:26-27, Paul writes that Christ washes the Church with water and the Word, to present her to himself as a radiant Bride. We are a vessel meant to contain the glory of God to the measure of the fullness of Christ (Eph. 2:20-22, 4:16). The process by which this occurs unfolds as you serve the Church with your spiritual gifts.

Missions and evangelism, therefore, are the means by which we make this temple, this vessel as large as possible to contain the glory of God. This is why all of us, even if we only "feel called" to local ministry, should long for and deploy resources toward the global advancement of the gospel. We should all desire that the Church grows and expands to the ends of the earth. Glory demands display. And so the Church, as the vessel of the glory of God, longs for and labors mightily toward the advancement of the gospel from sea to shining sea.

> For this reason I bow my knees to the Father of our Lord Jesus Christ, from whom the whole family in heaven and earth is named, that he would grant you, according to the riches of his glory, to be strengthened with might through his Spirit in the inner man, that Christ may dwell in your hearts through faith; that you, being rooted and grounded in love, may be able to comprehend with all the saints what is the width and length and depth and height—to know the love of Christ which passes knowledge; that you may be filled with all the fullness of God.
>
> Now to him who is able to do exceedingly abundantly above all that we ask or think, according to the power that works in us, to him be glory in the church by Christ Jesus to all generations, forever and ever. Amen. Ephesians 3:14-20

While many people view exercising their spiritual gifts as a means of finding a home, fitting in, and feeling useful in their local church, the whole point of spiritual gifts is far greater! In God's economy we are building a masterpiece, a mighty temple which contains the very presence of God, in which the power of God will flow through us, bringing life and healing to the nations. If we could only comprehend the width, the length, the depth and the height of the love God, we would be filled to the fullness of God (v.19). His power works in us so that Christ might be exalted throughout all generations (v.20).

I have heretofore ignored the *charismatic* controversies surrounding spiritual gifts because I feel so many people forget why they exist in the first place. Paul says it simply: for the common good (1 Corinthians 12:7). In other words, we are a humble part of something bigger, and our entire purpose is to make the whole Body function properly. (1 Corinthians 12: 14-20) Only a healthy, holy, spiritually mature Church can advance the gospel. And rightly so, we spend an almost inordinate amount of resource on keeping the ship from capsizing. We all bring our histories, our sinfulness, and our hang-ups to the local church. Much of our exercising of our spiritual gifts is designed to do very ordinary things like serving, teaching, encouraging, helping, showing mercy, and so forth (Romans 12:6-8).

What I am trying to emphasize is this: spiritual gifts are not like a carnival show, where we hype up the exercising of the spiritual gifts as the main attraction to our corporate worship meetings. We are helping each other get to a place of discipleship where we all serve each other in love, ministering to one another in prayer and the Word, and so grow to full maturity. Mature Christians bear fruit. The fruit that the Church bears because of your loving service accrues to your asset account. It's a beautiful thing.

If you resonate with the "why" of spiritual gifts, you will lean in and press on in the face of adversity to humbly exercise your spiritual gifts in the local church. While not going into detail on each spiritual gift, I do want to note that these are given as the Spirit determines, for the common good (1 Corinthians 12:11). In other words, I don't think you will "find" your spiritual gifts by taking an assessment. We discover our gifts as we serve in love. Paul, in fact encourages Christians to eagerly desire the greater gifts (1 Corinthians 12:31). Timothy received his gifts through the laying on of hands (1 Timothy 4:14). The Holy Spirit endows members of the Body to receive gifts to serve the Church as we eagerly serve the Church in love. Just like Peter and John preached with boldness before the Sanhedrin and the Holy Spirit filled Peter with wisdom and boldness to answer their questions, we too receive more of the Spirit as we walk forward in faith (Acts 4:8-13).

> *But you shall receive power when the Holy Spirit has come upon you; and you shall be witnesses to me in Jerusalem, and in all Judea and Samaria, and to the end of the earth. Acts 1:8*

A Few Additional Suggestions

1. Serve wherever your church needs, even if it is not in your gifting like watching toddlers or cleaning. The servant is not above his master. No task is too mundane for a Christ-servant.

2. Seek areas of responsibility that fill you with joy and passion. You will find that in those areas you will bless people around you. What may be difficult for others will feel completely effortless to you. I see this constantly with those who are gifted with "helps" and "mercy."

3. Serve in your gifting. Ask, seek, knock, and pray. Most likely there is no one at church thinking about how to best maximize your spiritual gifts. No matter. Be gracious. Keep trying. Be patient.

4. Mentor, especially cross-generational. Jr. High students help with grade school. Sr. High help with Jr. High and so on. Retirees reach out to professionals. Is this easy to do? No. But offer your services to your pastors and persist. Do it for the glory of God in his church and you will be blessed.

5. Pray constantly. Sing with joy and fervor. Isn't it interesting that when Paul writes about being filled with the Spirit those two activities are mentioned (Eph. 5:18 – 20, Eph. 6:18)?

6. Meditate on scripture. The sanctifying work of the Holy Spirit comes through the Word of God (John 17:17). I can't emphasize enough that the Holy Spirit himself works through his own words, far more than he does through circumstance.

Chapter 15 – ETERNAL ASSETS – The Kingdom

What is the Kingdom?

My kingdom is not of this world. John 18:36

The kingdoms of this world have become the kingdoms of our Lord and of his Christ, and He shall reign forever and ever! Revelation 11:15b

Too many people throw around phrases like "advance the kingdom" with little scriptural context. I come away from the everyday usage thinking that kingdom work means going to a fund-raiser for drilling wells in Africa. My intent and purpose in writing about the kingdom is not to exhaustively explain concepts like the "already, not yet" aspects of God's kingdom. My purpose is to stay within the context of how to grow eternal treasure. While not a treatise on the kingdom of God, it would be helpful to level set what scripture says about the kingdom. The implications of the definition of the kingdom will help us to apply our time, talent, and treasure toward fruitful endeavors, and thus advance his glory to the ends of the earth.

God's Sovereignty

The kingdom of God is everywhere and everything is under God's rule. In that expansive definition, the entire universe is under God's sovereignty. Nothing is outside of God's control (Isaiah 37:16). There is not a day that you and I wake up and God is caught by surprise. The tragedy of 9-11 did not catch God by surprise. He is not reacting to things. He is orchestrating all things, even as he himself is not tainted by the evil and sin that is part of the orchestration. In the expansive view of God's sovereignty, everything is under his rule.

> *My counsel shall stand, and I will accomplish all my purpose. Isaiah 46:10*
>
> *I form light and create darkness, I make well-being and create calamity, I am the Lord, who does all these things. Isaiah 45:7*
>
> *Whatever the Lord pleases, he does. Psalm 135:6*

He does according to his will among the host of heaven and among the inhabitants of the earth; and none can stay his hand or say to him, "What have you done?" Daniel 4:35

It is important that kingdom people begin with this truth, otherwise our kingdom building efforts feel like a futile task. Without the sovereignty of God, we will lose heart and give up. Churches are notoriously parochial and small minded. The resistance is great. After a few good attempts even the best give up. But when we trust in the sovereignty of God, we persist and persevere toward kingdom purposes.

God's Present Rule

A more narrow view of God's kingdom has to do with those who accept his rule. God is enthroned in the praises of Israel, his people (Psalm 22:3). In a practical sense, what is a king without subjects? And so the rebellious subjects are in a sense, outside of the kingdom, hence Christ's words, *"my kingdom is not of this world" (John 18:36).* The kingdom of God is within his people, among his people (Luke 17:21). The kingdom is a present reality that transformation occurs under God's rule and reign. Slowly, but surely the reality of justification works its way from the inside out.

So, kingdom building is first and foremost about increasing the number of subjects who will swear allegiance to the king of kings. That is why Jesus says, "All authority has been given to me...therefore, go." His authority deputizes the Church as his ambassadors to gather the nations to himself and draw all peoples into his kingdom. The process begins with conversion and continues through discipleship.

Go therefore and make disciples of all the nations, baptizing them in the name of the Father and of the Son and of the Holy Spirit, teaching them to observe all things that I have commanded you; and lo, I am with you always, even to the end of the age. Matthew 28:19-20

If Jesus is our king, then the Great Commission becomes our first priority. The Commission does not say, "Go make converts." The words state, "Go make disciples of all the nations." I sympathize with those who feel called to address local issues like urban blight, race relations, and inner city poverty and crime. I bless and support those efforts. But all kingdom people, regardless of present or specific calling, should have a longing for all the *ethne* – all the ethno-linguistic people groups of the world to bow at the feet of Christ. Jesus' heart cry yearns to bring all the nations into one people, his Bride, the Church.

Making disciples is kingdom business. It's tough work. This is not the same as getting people to raise their hands and ship them off to a six-week class. This is personal. If you are a kingdom person, your hands will get dirty from dealing with people's lives. Their lives are ugly. People are full of sin, full of history, full of hang ups. Discipleship is difficult so if your eye is not on the prize of Christ's kingdom, you will give up. Discipleship is life on life. But it is the main point of advancing the kingdom – bring people from all nations from darkness to light into fully devoted followers of Jesus Christ living out all of their time, talent, and treasure to the glory of God.

God's Leadership Influence

The kingdom of heaven is like a mustard seed, which a man took and sowed in his field, which indeed is the least of all the seeds; but when it is grown it is greater than the herbs and becomes a tree, so that the birds of the air come and nest in its branches. Matthew 13:31-32

Because Christians don't live in tiny communes, we live among lots and lots of non-Christians, our inside-out transformation will eventually be felt. We are called to be salt and light, a blessing to our communities. This shouldn't surprise us. We live out our lives in the community through 1,001 different professions. If we are working with all our might as unto the Lord, that excellence will permeate every facet of society. People should naturally be blessed by our very ordinary, kingdom living.

Our kingdom influence, then, is primarily experienced in our workplaces. Most adults spend the majority of their waking hours at work. If we live with excellence (not in competitive one upsmanship), we should naturally expect to see Christians eventually become elevated to higher and higher positions of authority in every legitimate sphere of influence.

Joseph and Daniel lived godly lives in pagan cultures, but because the Lord was with them and because they lived lives of excellence, their leadership and influence blessed their cultures. We should strive and endeavor to do the same in America.

This is not the same as, "Let's win the White House for the Republican Party and all will be well" kind of strategy. I know at this point the kingdom gets fuzzy in many people's minds. But if we start out with salvation, discipleship, living out our salvation with fear and trembling, then kingdom influence is yet another overflow from that. People of differing political views and alternate lifestyles should not fear this. Our integrity and excellence should bless them too. If you were a plumber, electrician, school teacher, or grocer, you would want all of your customers to receive an excellent experience, regardless of how they vote. We don't just do business with other Christians.

The dividing lines are only going to get sharper over the coming years and if we feel like our faith is getting beat up in the public square now, we should just hold on to our seats. It's going to get worse. Nonetheless, we should be committed to blessing those who hate us, despise us, and persecute us.

> *having your conduct honorable among the Gentiles, that when they speak against you as evildoers, they may, by your good works which they observe, glorify God in the day of visitation 1 Peter 2:12*

We need to turn the tide in our society, not by vilifying others, but by loving them. Sadly, evangelicals have contributed to the polarization in our society. Outspoken pundits who supposedly speak for evangelicals have anchored in the minds of many people that to be an evangelical means to be against something. God's kingdom is not a matter of debating politics on talk radio, but about the power of God (1 Corinthians 4:20). The gospel transforms us from the inside out and we live Spirit empowered lives in a lost and dying world. Our Spirit-filled influence permeates everything we touch, because we live out the excellence of the glory of God.

God's Future Reign
Of the increase of his government and peace there will be no end, Isaiah 9:7a

The Book of Ephesians spells out God's kingdom purpose. The kingdom is "already, but not yet."[37] The **already** is that in God's mind, in his timeless transcendence, all things are foreordained. Christ's death and triumphant resurrection secured the victory. The **not yet** is that 2,000 years later, the Church is advancing God's kingdom across the earth. **It is not yet because we're not yet done.**

> *In him we have redemption through his blood, the forgiveness of sins, according to the riches of his grace which he made to abound toward us in all wisdom and prudence, having made known to us the mystery of his will, according to his good pleasure which he purposed in himself, that in the dispensation of the fullness of the times he might*

---

[37] The term "already, but not yet" is credited to Gerhardus Vos, according to Wikipedia article "Kingdom Theology." Personally, I have not studied anything from Mr. Vos, but have heard this term used by several preachers including R.C. Sproul.

*gather together in one all things in Christ, both which are in heaven
and which are on earth—in him.*
Ephesians 1:7-10

In Ephesians the Apostle Paul introduces us to the Word "dispensation" or
"*oikonomia,*" God's economy. This dispensation is his glorious system of
rewards and incentives whereby he motivates the Church to labor toward
his purpose, the gathering of all *"ethne"* to one people, the Church.

Paul prays that God would open the eyes of our hearts to see the riches of
our inheritance in Christ (Ephesians 1:18). What is an inheritance? An
inheritance is our *kléronomeó,* our allotment, our shares in his estate. That
makes us shareholders, partakers, *koinonos* in his glory. What God in the
mystery of his will knew is that it would take an immense amount of
reward to motivate us because the amount of blood, sweat, and tears
required to advance the kingdom would be costly, just as Christ's sacrifice
was costly. But like Christ, we see past the suffering and run for the joy
ahead of us (Hebrews 12:2).

So what is the kingdom? The kingdom is the present and future reality of
people everywhere bowing to King Jesus. The effect of bending the knee to
King Jesus changes your heart. From your heart it changes your life. From
your life it changes your family and your church and your community.
From your community it changes your nation and your world. We bring
our circles of influence more and more into conformity of God's rule
through the discipleship process, both individually and corporately. And,
because God has given us work to do, to pay the bills, feed our families, and
live out our talents with passion, God's kingdom starts to influence society
through our integrity, our excellence, and our kindness toward others.

This process of bending the knee, winning souls to bend the knee, teaching
them to conform their lives to majesty of King Jesus continues with blood,
sweat, and tears until all the nations are gathered before Christ. And what
is crystal clear in the mind and mysteries of God will one day become a
crystal clear reality for everyone.

> *The kingdoms of this world have become the kingdoms of our Lord
> and of his Christ, and He shall reign forever and ever!*
> *Revelation 11:15*

Kingdom Work

Thy kingdom come. Thy will be done in earth, as it is in heaven.
Matthew 6:10 KJV

Therefore, kingdom work is the process by which we take the gospel to the nations so that all might have the opportunity to know, receive, and follow our great king. A key component of kingdom work is missions. Missions, then, is how we cross ethno-linguistic, cultural lines so that every knee should bow to King Jesus. Discipleship follows in which we help believers in the local church grow to full spiritual maturity, so that they might produce fruit for the gospel. And just as we channel tremendous resources for our own physical children to reach full potential in their time, talent, and treasure, so likewise we do the same for our spiritual children, brothers, and sisters all over the world.

Missions work does not stop at conversion. In order to sustain fruitfulness for new believers in the developing world, they need the same opportunities for education, health, and work to become fully devoted followers of Jesus Christ. This is not "social gospel." This is sustainable gospel. Imagine all of the women liberated from prostitution through gospel proclamation. Without tangible assistance in simple job training, these women will be back on the street in sexual slavery.

We should not create a dividing line between what we view as proclamation and compassion. Compassion should not stop at just enough aid and relief necessary to "pray the prayer." Compassionate, kingdom work will take an inordinate amount of time, talent, and treasure from the older brothers in the Western Church to create the conditions for sustainable fruitfulness.

And, although the temptation certainly exists for sustainable development to degrade into gospel-less social justice, it need not be so. The resources exist in the West to do both. Just as we view fruitfulness for our own children means developing them to self-sustainment, so also we need to train the indigenous church to "fish" and not just hand them the "fish" of our monthly checks. We move past digging wells **for** Africans to digging wells **with** Africans. We train up indigenous pastors and leaders who will steward their own churches and countries out of corruption and toward sustainable spiritual and economic growth. Think of the sheer amount of resources required for our physical children to grow to their full potential, to stand on their own two feet and be fruitful. That's the kind of investment that we need to consider for our sister churches around the world.

None of this will be easy. Completing our mission on earth will require more than the trifle giving of our time, talent, and treasure from the American Church. What is required goes far beyond one week short term missions trips. What is required is a sustained effort multiple times over what we are doing today.

"David, David, what exactly should we be doing" I don't have all the answers. What I love about this idea of building equity is that equity owners are rarely given a manual on how to increase their value. By analogy, millions of immigrants to America successfully started their own business on the simple belief that if they combined hard work with providing good products and services, they could grow equity wealth for themselves. Very few of them go to business school and yet the dream of growing equity results in innovation, creativity, hard work, and sustained effort. So here's my answer: Go all out for the glory of God and build up your heavenly equity. Faithfulness and fruitfulness will lead to kingdom work.

What we are doing today in the Church is a 1% effort to advance the kingdom. We are seeing insufficient innovation and creativity to complete the Great Commission because, I believe too many Christians don't care about their heavenly treasure. When I look at the massive innovation entrepreneurs generate in search of earthly wealth creation, I am convinced that treasure and glory are at the heart of it.[38] Where our treasure is, there our hearts will be also. Therefore, I am convinced that by placing our treasure in heaven, we can see similar innovation. With a sustained and concerted effort of kingdom work, we could complete the Great Commission in our lifetime.

> *For thine is the kingdom and the power and the glory forever, Amen.*
> *Matthew 6:13 KJV*

---

[38] Think of Google, Amazon, Microsoft, Apple, General Electric and so on. At the end of the day, the innovation they generate is to advance the glory of their own name, their brand.

Chapter 16 – ETERNAL ASSETS – The Path of Wisdom

For which of you, desiring to build a tower, does not first sit down and count the cost, whether he has enough to complete it? Luke 14:28 ESV

So how do we balance the amount of effort we spend in our own spiritual development versus what is multiplied in other people's lives? I would like to offer a simple way to think about sequencing your efforts.

1. Get clarity on the glory of God. At the end of the day, if our efforts are not for the glory of God, we receive ZERO credit.

2. Work up the stack beginning with the Word of God.

    a. If fruit is ultimately overflow from the heart, then the heart must change by the power of the Holy Spirit. The Holy Spirit illuminates our mind, convicts us of sin, and brings about a *metanoia*, a change of mind. That change of mind results in changed priorities, changed passions, and changed actions.

    b. Next work on your own godly character. You can't export what doesn't work. Even Paul worried that he himself would be disqualified from the race (1 Corinthians 9:27). What credit is that to you if you preach the gospel for 69 years and then in the 70th year experience a tremendous and public moral failure? Avoid doing foolish things that would disgrace our Lord.

    c. Invest in those closest to you, your spouse, your children, your friends, and your spiritual offspring. Most likely, the majority of your time, talent, and treasure will be invested in your own family's fruitfulness.

    d. Serve the church. Do it as a family! Model serving others in the church to your children. Faith is a team sport and you will experience real synergy. Other people will come into your life and give you capacity that you could never supply on your own. You will do the same for others. When the church works, it's a beautiful thing.

3. Your life will experience ebbs and flows in different cadences: daily, weekly, and seasons of life. Don't despise any of the seasons you are in. Don't let guilt drive your decisions. There will be seasons where you will be very involved with your church. Other seasons you will need to focus on family. You will need wisdom to guide you. The Word of God and prayer continue to be foundational to how you apply your time.

4. As God increases your capacity, serve in a kingdom capacity. Think Big Church beyond your local church. Although the Church divides herself along every imaginable line, **your heart should long for unity.** Be a peacemaker even as you hold up the mighty standard of truth. Actively reach across denominational and congregational lines. Stretch your faith and use all of your overflowing treasure to advance the gospel to the ends of the earth. Create the conditions for fruitfulness in the Church around the world.

So how do we increase fruit?
The Path of Wisdom

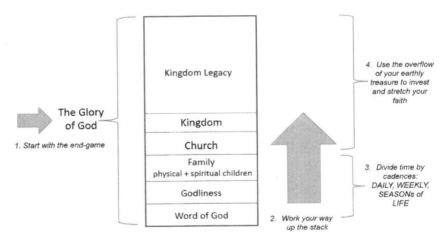

Is it worth it?

Ye know that your labor is not in vain in the Lord. 1 Corinthians 15:58b KJV

God is protecting my heavenly treasure! He knows that I am so full of folly, vanity, and arrogance that seeing results would cause me to hog the credit. In God's economy the only boasting allowed is boasting in the Lord. So in hiding results of our labors from us God demonstrates that he cares about our eternal treasure more than we do! I can imagine our heavenly Father, full of delight, eagerly waiting to lavish recognition, reward, and responsibility above all we can ask or imagine. In this life, it is enough to know we are but servants just doing our duty (Luke 17:10). But in the next life, we will see, it was all worth it.

Our labor is not in vain! The way of the cross will be full of heartache, loneliness, and questions. God promises an immense return for the investment so that we continue on. When you are struggling with seeing fruit and want to give up, your faith will tell you, "It's worth it. Press on." Just because we do not always see fruit does not mean that the fruit is not present. And like a good farmer, **we focus on all the factors in our control: soil and seed**. We till, fertilize, and water the soil. We plant good seed and let God do the rest. He will bring both fruit and growth for his own glory. In God's economy, **God is the one who brings the increase.**

> *And let us not grow weary while doing good, for in due season we shall reap if we do not lose heart. Galatians 6:9*

Part 4

Liabilities: Resources God Entrusts

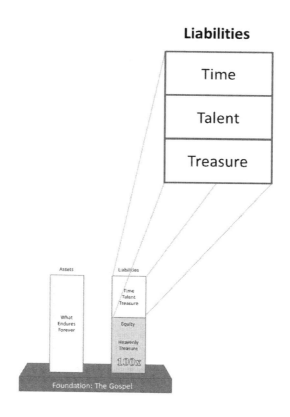

Chapter 17 – LIABILITIES – Overview
Time, Talent, and Treasure – Why did God give us those?

So teach us to number our days so that we may gain a heart of wisdom. Psalm 90:12

In God's economy the Lord gives us temporary resources to build eternal assets. However, if you were to calculate how much we focus on the liability column, how much focus would you say you give to the eternal asset column versus the liability column? I would hazard to say we spend over 90% of our time, talent, and treasure on building and maintaining our time, talent, and treasure. **Our lives are primarily spent in the liability column.** I believe one major reason why is that most evangelicals believe that life is about "success first, then significance." Meaning, I can focus on me and my success now and at some point I can give thought to the Lord. Can you imagine going to your bank every year for 70 years, get a bigger and bigger loan just to brag how big of a loan you've taken out and have no plan on what to do with the money? But, if we are to live in the knowledge and fear of the Lord, we would realize that Christ is significant NOW, and so we cannot delay in investing in what's eternal.

The process of building up our liability column

How and why does this focus on the liability column occur? When our children are young, they have nothing but time. Time is immaterial to them. Days blend from one play time to another. In the course of time, as we begin to mature in our physical and intellectual capabilities, our parents train us up in the way we should go (Proverbs 22:6) as good parents do. That means they begin this intense period of educational development and experience management. This process from K – 12 is focused on maximizing the innate talents of children.

The process of growing talent is also called *human capital* development. In economic terms human capital is the potential to generate financial capital. How does this work? Our children first acquire knowledge. Knowledge is quite simply that which is learned vicariously through books, videos, and lectures. Knowledge gets converted into experience. Experience plus practice form skill. Skill levels stack on top of each other and become complex skills. With enough practice and focus (the rule of thumb is 10,000 hours), we gain true skill or mastery of a particular subject.

What our economy pays for is skill. Skill is ultimately the ability to solve an employer's problems, invent compelling products, serve customers, and the like. The process by which skill, or human capital becomes financial capital is called *monetization.* The market monetizes or pays us for delivering the value of our skill.

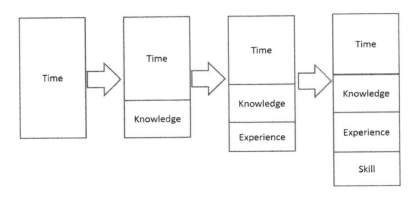

Somewhere between the ages of 26 and 30 we reach our peak human capital potential. Our minds are sharp. Our ideas are full of hope and vibrancy. We tackle problems with zest. Between 30 and 45 we rapidly convert that human capital into wealth and somewhere between ages 45 and 55 the time value of money kicks in and we realize the benefits of our investment in human capital, even while that human capital (our brains/health) fades. In the retirement years, we seek to live off of our created wealth and still maintain enough to transfer to future generations and the kingdom. We spend a significant portion of our treasure on maintaining our human capital (our health). At that point, we start asking ourselves, "How can I go from success to significance?" This is the current paradigm in the world.

Monetizing Skill

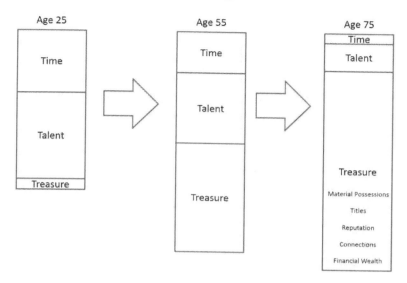

If you live by the power of the Holy Spirit, Jesus said, "Out of his heart will flow rivers of living water." In God's economy, Christ is our significance, period. Believing this is key to breaking the paradigm of "success first, then significance." The paradigm I'd like to suggest is **"Grow, Invest."** Grow your liabilities, but immediately and constantly reinvest in the kingdom, the asset column of the eternal balance sheet.

Here's what the Bible says about time. You're not guaranteed any more time than TODAY. The "success to significance" paradigm assumes you will live to age 80. So, although the Bible exhorts good planning, it also reminds us that God is judging us for the fruit we produce today, **now.**

> *He who had received the five talents* ***went at once*** *and traded with them, and he* ***made five talents more****. Matthew 25:16*

So, for the rest of this book, I will describe the process by which we can both grow our earthly resource base according to our stages of life, but also **not delay** in **investing** in what counts for eternity.

Chapter 18 – GROW AND INVEST – Stage 1
Forming Character & Talent

*For bodily exercise profits a little, but **godliness is profitable** for all things, having promise of the life that now is and of that which is to come.*
1 Timothy 4:8

For parents it may be tempting to view the time we have our children under our stewardship as primarily about setting them up for SUCCESS in this lifetime. Indeed, if you spend any length of time with most parents, the chatter focuses on the road to success. Parents obsess about schooling, sports, life experiences – it seems like college prep begins at kindergarten. Is it any wonder that these children grow up guided by this "success to significance" paradigm? In order to teach them to grow heavenly treasure, we parents need to organize our stewardship of their development around what is eternal.

Salvation and the Word

I find it fascinating how many parents I talk to who aren't believers, and yet baptize their children. They themselves do not believe in the lordship of Jesus Christ, yet somehow are compelled either by upbringing or fear of uncertainty that they should have their kids baptized. So from the start many children's faith journey resembles a nice side-show, but the real focus is on earthly success.

Similarly, many evangelicals view the Sinner's Prayer like a task to complete. Rather than spend the time discipling their children in the love and fear of the Lord, many parents outsource their children's spiritual growth to their church. While I believe that some children demonstrate saving faith when they pray the Sinner's Prayer, I can tell you after reading hundreds of membership testimonies that for a large majority, reciting the Sinner's Prayer is like a check the box activity. Rather than follow up and follow through, too many parents think their child is "good," and that the eternal salvation issue is at rest. Back to the road to success....

Should we assume that our child is "good?" I've talked to many parents who in the course of fretting over their child's wayward faith journey assure me that their child is "good" because they prayed the prayer. In Romans 1:15, Paul declares to the Church in Rome his desire to preach the gospel to the church, to those who have already received Christ. The gospel never gets old. Instead of focusing exclusively on behaviors, the heart issue of Christ's lordship is the first place to start.

Eternity is too important to view salvation as checking some box. Indeed, in saving faith we pass from death to life, but salvation is a work of the Holy Spirit. Our responsibility as parents is to diligently teach sound doctrine in the Word of God, keep preaching the gospel, and model a vibrant faith. We focus on soil and seed. In doing so, God in his sovereignty will awaken the dead soul through his power and by his Word call that son or daughter to himself. Although parents are not decisive in our children's fruitfulness, (the Holy Spirit is), we are instrumental to the Spirit's work.

I remember as a young child waking up at 5:00AM and walking over to my parents' room. They were often on the floor, prostrate in prayer, calling out to God in prayer. Or I would see them reading, memorizing, and meditating on scripture. This image was burned in my mind, and has formed a model for me today. So when my little children get up early and come downstairs, they will see me studying scripture and praying. Often they will crawl into my lap as I read and I tell them, "This is the most important thing I can teach you. Study and love the Word of God!"

What does it look like to improve the soil of your children's hearts? After modeling your own devotion to the Word of God, teach it to your children. We use devotionals like Long Story Short which teach kids directly from scripture. As much as I used to love the kids' Bible story books with the pictures of Noah and the animals smiling as they pop their heads out of the ark, we have to stop treating the Bible like it's a fairy tale book. Some parents are worried about the frank and adult topics the Bible uses and think they are "protecting" their kids with "family friendly" watered down kids' books. Jesus said, *"Let the children come to me, and do not hinder them, for to such belongs the kingdom of God" (Luke 18:16 ESV)*. By the power of the Holy Spirit, the Word of God is the only means of regenerating the human heart. **It is not something to protect our kids from!** Yes, the Bible is "mature" content. Dying on a cross is "mature" content. Learning biblical "mature" content is how our children put off childish ways.

Additionally, as parents we need to use the Bible as reference for every problem we deal with. How should our kids relate to other kids in the neighborhood? *"Be ye kind to one another, tenderhearted, forgiving one another" (Ephesians 4:32 KJV)*. How should our children apply themselves at school? *"All hard work brings a profit, but mere talk leads only to poverty" (Proverbs 14:23 NIV)*. How should they handle self-esteem issues? *"I will praise you, for I am fearfully and wonderfully made" (Psalm 139:14)*. We could go on and on but you get the point.

"All scripture is God breathed and is useful for teaching, rebuking, correcting and training in righteousness." 2 Timothy 3:16 NIV

After modeling and instilling a love for God, a love for his Word, and devotion to prayer, we as parents should focus on character development.

Your Children's Development

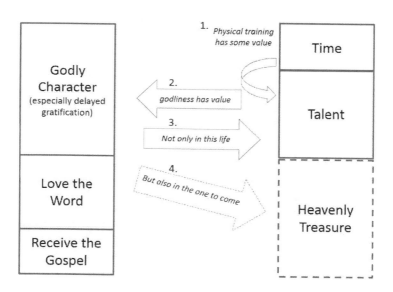

The Fruit of the Spirit is...Self-Control

There is a famous study that was conducted at Stanford on the merits of delayed gratification. It is commonly known as the "marshmallow experiment." In the study researchers took young children into a room and put a marshmallow in front of them. "If you don't eat the marshmallow now, we'll give you two later!" The researchers left the room for 15 minutes and observed the child's behavior on camera. When you watch the videos of this experiment it is quite humorous. The children contort, squirm, cover their eyes, and do all sort of coping strategies to try to exercise self-control. Only one-third waited long enough to get the reward.

What is interesting from this famous study is that the researchers followed up on the children decades later and found that the ones who delayed gratification the longest were the most successful in almost every measurable attribute of life, health, emotional wellbeing, and education level.

Isn't it interesting that the Bible says that "godliness has value in this life and in the life to come?" Because we often put spiritual in the "other" category, we tend to undervalue spiritual disciplines with our children and overvalue education, sports, and life experience. So many parents tell me that they believe the secret to their children's future success lay with putting as many varied life experiences in front of them as they can. Could it be true that some parents are crafting Harvard entrance applications a decade in advance?

Where in college entrance applications do you demonstrate self-denial and delayed gratification? There is no *"captain of the delayed gratification club"* title that you can put on your list of accomplishments. Therefore, we tend to overindulge our children in activity after activity so that we can build up a resume of accomplishments. And yet, godliness has value in this life and in the life to come. **Godliness** not only is **practical**, but it is **practice** for the **assignment** our heavenly Father will give us in the next life.

> *...teaching us that, denying ungodliness and worldly lusts, we should live soberly, righteously, and godly in the present age, looking for the blessed hope and glorious appearing of our great God and Savior Jesus Christ. Titus 2:12-13*

As parents, one of the most important lessons we can teach our children, after loving God and the Word, is character development, especially to exercise delayed gratification. The entire essence of God's economy is delayed gratification. Godliness is not asceticism. We don't hate pleasure as if pleasure itself were evil. We are saying "No" now for a greater "Yes" later.

Your children are not kids. They are adults in training, meaning we are preparing them for the adult world. Only in recent years has the concept of adolescence (endless delay of adulthood) taken form in popular culture. But if the goal of life is to bear fruit in the eternal asset column, the best time to start is when the habits of godliness can be quickly absorbed and ingrained. Do old dogs learn new tricks? Start young.

Other Suggestions

There are so many ways to invest in your children's future that will reap huge fruit in the long run. Allow me to suggest a few:

1. AWANA: The Bible verses my brain has retained into adulthood are what I learned as a child in AWANA, in King James Version by the way. Now, everything I memorize rapidly dissipates. Invest in a love for the Bible at a young age!

2. Hospitality: My children are the best, most natural evangelists. When we invite guests, my kids always volunteer to pray before the meal. My kids talk about faith without any fear or hesitation and guests aren't threatened. Let your kids practice evangelism in the context of hospitality.

3. Serve in the church together. Worship together. Not to be trite, but, "Monkey see, monkey do." If you're not modeling a vibrant faith, how are your children to catch what you don't have? In serving the church together, you can appraise their service and encourage their budding spiritual gifts.

4. Generosity: I learned generosity watching my parents. When I go to charity events, this seems to be the pattern. Almost everyone I meet at giving events started young. This is very difficult to learn at an old age. Personally, we give our kids money almost every Sunday to put in the offering plate just to practice the discipline of generosity. If our kids want to give everything in their piggy bank, we encourage it. <u>You don't have to teach stinginess</u>. Use words like "invest" not "give away" as you explain how money circulates for kingdom purposes. When we "give away" our money, we are saying that worshiping God through offerings is a "loss," exactly the opposite of God's economy.

5. Missions: There are many families that go on missions trips together. I can think of no better way to instill a love for advancing the kingdom than going together. Brainstorm about their future in terms of kingdom impact using the gifts God has given them. They are part of the mission. We pray over friends and neighbors together. We are on mission together. We don't send them on church buses to go do things we ourselves would not do. Don't you find it interesting that for sports like football the kids are practicing what the adults are doing? In church world, it seems like the

opposite. No. Missions is what the adults should be doing and the children should learn from the adults.

Chapter 19 – GROW and INVEST – Stage 2
Finding Your Life's Profession

Train up a child in the way he should go and when he is old he will not depart from it. Proverbs 22:6

Here's a contrarian spin to the entire subject of career management. The Bible is indifferent to your career choice. The verses we will look at are indifferent on **"what"** career path to take. The Bible focuses a lot of detail on the **"why"** (for the glory of God) and **"how"** (with all your might) of work. [See Colossians 3:17 and 1 Corinthians 10:31] Looking at the eternal balance sheet, this should be obvious: our earthly careers are temporary, but our godly character and kingdom impact are eternal.

Go with the grain

What does it mean to train up a child "in the way he should go?" I'd like to suggest two pathways: One, the "way" is God's way. Narrow is the way of Christ. So, we should train our children to follow Christ in the way of the cross. The way of the cross is servant-leadership. We lead by serving. We give. We practice at a young age putting others first. None of this comes instinctively to children. Young children instinctively say, "Mine! Mine!" or, "Because I want to."

Training up godly character is key to building up heavenly treasure. Why? In the previous chapter I wrote how practicing delayed gratification leads to earthly success. Indeed, if you practice godly disciplines, which are "profitable in this life," then it should not surprise you that hard work, integrity, team orientation will result in success. Just by focusing on growing eternal fruit, you will set up your children for earthly success.

However, if parents are not intentional in teaching a servant's orientation, earthly success will lead to arrogance. Success is a double-edged sword. Success is both a blessing from God and a test from God (Deuteronomy 8:17). Too much success leads to pride. Too much pride leads to a downfall. So, in the "way he should go" means to first of all, follow Christ's example.

The second part of training "in the way he should go" is to focus on natural talents and inclinations. Maximizing talent requires sheer focused effort,

10,000 hours to be exact.[39] To be a chess master, a prima-ballerina, a professional athlete, or a subject matter expert you need 10,000 hours of practice. Practice makes perfect. Skill is what eventually gets rewarded in a market-based economy.

> *Do you see a man skilled in his work? He will stand before kings. He will not serve before obscure men. Proverbs 22:29*

Mastering any skill takes a phenomenal amount of practice and patience. The reason why most people do not focus on gaining mastery in any particular area is this: unless you are naturally passionate about the subject, you will give up. You will burn out. 10,000 hours is a long time and a lot of practice and you will only follow through if you love what you're doing. (And I don't mean 10,000 hours of "mailing it in" if you know what I mean).

> *And Jesus increased in wisdom and stature, and in favor with God and men. Luke 2:52*

As far as the scripture record tells us, Jesus did what his parents told him to do. As far as we can tell in scripture, Jesus grew up in the same town his whole life and learned directly from his father Joseph the carpentry trade. No obsessing about living in the right neighborhood with the right school district, no obsessing about what activities and sports to be engaged in, no obsessing about what circle of friends to hang out in, Jesus grew in the knowledge of scripture, and in a profession his earthly father taught.

Was it the "perfect profession, the perfect job?" Probably not. Was Paul's profession of being a tentmaker the ideal job? Probably not. Was Peter's profession of being a fisherman the perfect job? Probably not. We obsess a lot about these questions, but the Bible does not spend a lot of time on them. And so, we extrapolate quite a lot from Proverbs 22:6 and try to interpret "in the way he should go" to the nth-degree. Here's my take: Simply find something you love to do and get really good at it. The market pays for true skill, mastery. In the meantime, focus on what is eternal, Jesus-like character. God prepared us for "works" (Ephesians 2:10). So let's stop obsessing about the perfect assignment and start working for the glory of his name. Get going!

---

[39] I highly suggest reading the book <u>Outliers</u> by Malcolm Gladwell to fully understand the concept of 10,000 hours of practice leading to mastery.

Character vs. Talent

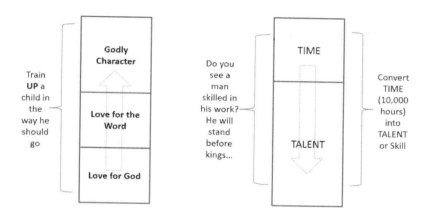

The Bible is Indifferent about Career Paths

Where in the Bible does it speak about career being a calling? In our everyday usage, we have elevated career to such a lofty goal, that we start using terms like "calling" in conjunction with it. This adds unnecessary stress and heartache over college selection, choice of major, and subsequent job applications. Are those decisions really motivated out of bearing fruit for the sake of the glory of God?

What does the Bible say about "calling?"

> Moreover whom He predestined, these He also called; whom **he called**, these He also **justified;** and whom He justified, these He also glorified. Romans 8:30

> For the gifts and the **calling** of God are irrevocable. Romans 11:29

> But you are a chosen generation, a royal priesthood, a holy nation, his own special people, that you may proclaim the praises of him who **called you** out of darkness **into his marvelous light.** 1 Peter 2:9

> For God did not **call us** to uncleanness, but **in holiness.** 1 Thessalonians 4:7

We are to press on toward the prize of the upward call (Philippians 3:14), walk in a manner worthy of the call (Ephesians 4:1) and take hold of eternal life to which we were called (1 Timothy 6:12). In other words, calling is about God's election, salvation, and work of sanctification in our lives. These are all on the eternal assets column of the balance sheet.

Could it be that our elevation of career as calling is because we are all subtly narcissists? We all think highly of our glory, our fame, our reputation and that career, titles, and corner offices validate our choices? Therefore, we place an exorbitant amount of energy and focus on titles and career management. But when the Bible speaks of careers, there is an air of indifference.

> And **whatever you do** in word or deed, do all in the name of the Lord Jesus, giving thanks to God the Father through Him. Colossians 3:17

> And **whatever you do,** do it heartily, as to the Lord and not to men. Colossians 3:23

> Therefore, whether you eat or drink, or **whatever you do,** do all to the glory of God. 1 Corinthians 10:31

The Bible continually focuses us on what is eternal and puts into perspective our obsession with success. Everything is for the Lord. We like to throw around phrases like, "I'm living for the glory of God," but until you start converting those temporal resources into eternal assets, I'm sorry to say the record will show that you were living for your own glory. Your calling is to be saved. Your calling is to holiness. Your calling is to Christlikeness, to servanthood. There are specific callings in serving the Church.

> So Christ himself gave the apostles, the prophets, the evangelists, the pastors and teachers, to equip his people for works of service, so that the Body of Christ may be built up until we all reach unity in the faith and in the knowledge of the Son of God and becoming mature, attaining to the whole measure of the fullness of Christ. Ephesians 4:11-13 NIV

These are your calling in the church. **Outside of full-time ministry, the Bible never refers to your career as your calling**. Work is your assignment, your mission field, your training ground for godliness, and your opportunity to generate resources to invest in eternal impact. Yes, build up those resources. If those resources stagnate in the liability column, you show that you are living for your own glory. If those resources flow like "rivers of living water" into eternal assets, then you are living for the glory of God.

Chapter 20 – GROW and INVEST – Stage 3
Fruitful for the Kingdom

...redeeming the time, because the days are evil. Galatians 5:16

What I've been proposing is a "GROW and INVEST" framework. Grow your earthly time, talent, and treasure but simultaneously invest those elements into the Word, godliness, discipleship, all things that last for eternity. The stage that seems to take Christians (especially men) into a long black hole occurs between post-college and retirement. Chasing the American Dream can squander your best years for the kingdom. In this chapter, I'd like to offer some practical ideas to help you continually reinvest into your eternal assets while balancing the day-to-day aspects of making a living.

I remember when I was asked to be an elder at my church. My wife and I had three young children and I was very busy traveling for work. But we loved our church and wanted to support it so I prayed to God, "Lord, you know my heart. You know that I want to build your church and for my marriage and family to flourish. Would you please give me favor?" I prayed a version of that prayer every day. You know what? God honored that prayer. I didn't overwork. We experienced the best years of my business career ever in terms of results, teamwork, and memories. And we were able to invest more time, talent, and treasure in God's church and kingdom.

So here are the two vectors of grow-invest. The first is in your liability account and the second is in your eternal asset column.

Grow Your Resources (for the Kingdom)
Follow my example, as I follow the example of Christ. 1 Corinthians 11:1 NIV

If you view your liability accounts as resources for the kingdom, then by all means, make as much money as humanly possible. I know many godly men who demonstrate both earthly success and simultaneous spiritual growth. To give you a narrative that may help you visualize the process, I'd like to tell you about my friend Bobby.

Bobby was a young salesman who did not fit well in large corporate structures. He found such structures stifling so he decided to start his own company. Bob thought, "What if I could start a business based on biblical principles? Could that work in the real world?" So, for the next decade he built a very successful technology company. Bob grew the company by putting in his 10,000 hours of simply outhustling, outselling his competitors. He and his colleagues honed and perfected their offering by being the best customer focused company in their industry. Demonstrating *delayed gratification,* Bob refused to allow the culture to get cocky or arrogant. He continually reinvested profits into growing the business to stay ahead of the competition. Their reputation for quality and customer service eventually snowballed until the company grew to become one of the largest technology value-added-resellers in the country.

GROW – INVEST Framework

Finally, a mega conglomerate acquired Bob's company for a very attractive price and Bob was able to monetize his investment. Did Bob go from success to significance? No, during this entire period of growth he continually poured his life into the eternal asset column.

Not to brag on Bob, but during the exponential growth trajectory at work, he served as a church elder, taught at AWANA, led many colleagues to Christ, grew a ministry in Haiti, and served in numerous other ministries. He and his beautiful wife Jennifer adopted two kids from Haiti and grew their family size to five children. Jennifer taught women's Bible studies while managing the schedules of their incredibly talented children.

Bob and Jennifer simultaneously grew their resource base and the kingdom. How? Sheer dependence on the Holy Spirit. They prayed. They did not neglect reading the Word of God. Instead of living in fear and hoarding, they let their time, talent, and treasure continually flow toward building up eternal assets. In other words, **when you are single-minded in your devotion to Christ, growing the business, raising a family, and advancing the kingdom are all part of the same thing.**

Bob and Jen (and many others I might add) demonstrate that living for Christ need not be an either/or proposition. I'm either in full-time ministry or I'm making money in the marketplace. No. This is a false choice. Christ comes first in all areas and the lordship of Christ touches all areas of life.

> *But we have this treasure in jars of clay to show that this all-surpassing power is from God and not from us. 2 Corinthians 4:7 NIV*

So how do you grow your resource base? *Whatever you do, work with all your might as unto the Lord and not for men.* Whether you are a Christian or not, to succeed in your profession you have to work at it with all your might. As Christians, we have to work hard and live with honesty, integrity, and humility. By creating useful products, providing high levels of service, being responsive to customers and your employer, doing it with high integrity will be rewarded in this life. Working at a trade, any trade with all diligence will eventually produce mastery. Mastery is what the market pays for and your earthly resource base grows. So, what determines whether you are living for the glory of God? What do you do with all that resource you've accumulated? If resources stay in the liability column, it is all for your glory. If resources flows to the other side, then your efforts were not a waste from a kingdom perspective.

Invest in Eternal Impact

At the same time, you can invest time and talent in what is eternal. Having a full-time job does not give men or women a hall pass to delay obedience to the gospel until retirement. Here are some other practical suggestions for what you can do to invest in eternal fruit at the workplace:

1. Be excellent. Work as unto the Lord. Just working with excellence, will elevate the quality of your work and customers, colleagues, and your boss will notice. Although you ultimately work for the Lord, you have a fiduciary responsibility to your employer who is cutting your check. Be excellent in all things.

2. Pray over your colleagues every day as you drive to work. Mentally rehearse your interactions and pray that you would act in a God-glorifying manner. Bless them, especially the colleagues who annoy you.

3. Guard your lips at work, especially at the water cooler. Don't get dragged into the muck of complaining. I know it's every American's right to complain, but stop. It is a sin. Philippians 2:14-15 exhort us to "Do everything without complaining...so that you will prove yourselves to be blameless and innocent, children of God." Be positive always, you will stand out.

4. Raise your faith flag. Whether it's praying before you eat or weaving your faith life into your personal narrative, or simply explaining that you went to church during the weekend, it should not be a shock that you are a Christian. Set aside evangelizing for a moment. Shouldn't it be completely normal that you are who you are? Shouldn't it be completely natural that the fruit that abounds in your life naturally show up without sounding contrived and forced? You just are a Christian. Don't hide it.

5. Invite your colleague friends over for dinner. Let them see your kids running around. Let them see you pray before meals. Let them see your unvarnished life. Neighbors and colleagues always ask about how we raise our kids. This is another perfect opportunity to explain the hope that you have in Christ, with gentleness and meekness. A home cooked meal drops all defenses and screams authenticity. Be authentic. You don't have to hand them a decision card at dessert time.

6. Prepare for that faith conversation. Buy the Navigators' Topical Memory System and memorize those verses! Scripture needs to be top of mind. Know the Romans Road. Our minds need to be able retrieve scripture easily. At least know the references: Romans 3:23, Romans 6:23, Ephesians 2:8-9, John 3:16, Titus 3:5, and so forth. To do the work of an evangelist takes work and preparation for that slim chance your colleague will open up and let you share about Christ. Prepare for the faith conversation like it's going to happen, because if you do, it will.

7. Be generous and thoughtful at key points in your colleagues' lives. These are high points and low points where you can genuinely and authentically share your faith and share in their joy and sorrow.

Think weddings, funerals, births, and the like. Be genuine and empathize. This is not the time to preach.

8. Open doors and step in to the faith conversation: Don't panic! If you've done points #1 – 7, I promise you, you will have the vital conversation about your faith in Jesus Christ. Make it instinctive and talk about the historical Jesus. We so quickly jump into (needless) arguments about politics, about world religion, about evolution and global warming, about every topic except Jesus. I go straight to talking about his life, death, and resurrection. Plant the seed and let the Holy Spirit bring about fruit.

9. Pray for your colleagues. Once you broach the topic of salvation you have to believe and trust that "Faith comes from hearing the message and the message through the Word of God." You've done your part. Trust God will do his.

10. Maintain your integrity. What's great about evangelism is that you become incredibly aware of the importance of your witness at work. What a wonderful, sanctifying mechanism to enable you to produce more fruit! You will conscientiously work harder, with a positive attitude, and treat your colleagues with dignity and respect because you won't want to destroy your witness. Being intentional and strategic about advancing the gospel at work will bring more fruit.

Every Christian can take these steps, regardless of present assignment. But what if you feel that nagging sense that you need to move on? What should you do?

Stretch your vision for work

For the entrepreneurs and inventors, get a vision for how your talent can serve humanity. Creating the conditions for human flourishing is part of advancing God's kingdom. I find most evangelicals never give it a second thought about aligning the content of their work with the kingdom of God. We may be tempted to focus on the End-Times and exhibit pessimism about creating conditions for human fruitfulness. I've heard too many "It's like rearranging the chairs on the deck of the Titanic analogies" in my life. Listen, I get it. If you believe (like I do) that we can hasten the day of the Lord through missions and evangelism you might be confused about this. What's the point of doing anything else besides winning souls? The answer comes in the book of Jeremiah.

Marry and have sons and daughters; find wives for your sons and
give your daughters in marriage, so that they too may have sons and
daughters. Increase in number there; do not decrease. Also, seek the
peace and prosperity of the city to which I have carried you into exile.
Pray to the LORD for it, because if it prospers, you too will prosper.
Jeremiah 29:6-7

Like the ancient Israelites were exiles and sojourners in Babylon, a land of
false gods and idolatry, we too are citizens of another country just passing
through. Why in the world would God command the Israelites to pray for
the peace and prosperity of Babylon, whose evil king had just slaughtered
thousands of Hebrews?

The answer is that we carry within us the kingdom of God. The kingdom is
here, but not in its full power. The kingdom is here, but it's also coming.
Until the kingdom comes in full power, we are supposed to live fruitful,
productive lives where we make disciples of the nations and be a blessing
to all who surround us.

You are the light of the world. A city set on a hill cannot be hidden.
Nor do people light a lamp and put it under a basket, but on a stand,
and it gives light to all in the house. In the same way, let your light
shine before others, so that they may see your good works and give
glory to your Father who is in heaven. Matthew 5:14-16

I remember going on a missions trip to Kenya. Thousands of people
responded to an invitation to receive Christ. As we were hopping on our
buses, going back to our comfy lives in America, I asked one of the Kenyan
pastors what they needed most. "Jobs" he said without missing a beat.
With 50% unemployment, you can't even begin to understand the kind of
structural sin that gets perpetuated because people are not gainfully
employed. Men sit around, get drunk all day and fornicate and get women
pregnant. Women, desperate to take care of their children enter into a life
of prostitution. Because of all the unprotected sex, AIDS has become a
pandemic affecting men, women, and children. Many parents die and leave
children as orphans. The orphans have no education or family and became
street children. Many of them become prostitutes or criminals because
there's nothing else for them to do. Must I go on?

Don't you find it ironic that we Americans are constantly spiking the ball in
the proverbial end zone after our missions trips and patting ourselves on
the back about how many souls were saved? Don't you find it
disconcerting? I do. I want millions of people to know Jesus Christ like you

do. But don't we have any vision for them to live out their lives for the glory of God after they are saved? That means after they are saved, our spiritual children don't have to go back to a life of prostitution. After they are saved they have opportunities for education and jobs. After they are saved, they have the ability to become productive members of their own society, make money, and support their own local churches. Shouldn't we want them to be self-supportive and not constantly waiting for us to throw them our spare change?[40] Where's the dignity in that? I know you care because if these were your own children and grandchildren, the thought of them growing up in horrendously filthy conditions like our spiritual children, brothers, and sisters live in would make you mad as hell.

Guess what we have in America? We have the largest marketplace on the planet. We have endless capacity to import. We have the best management, deepest expertise on product design, product management, most sophisticated manufacturing, logistics, and know-how for import/export, etc. I have a vision that millions of Baby Boomers would use their immense talents and treasure to help transformation take place in the inner city and around the world. I have a vision that millions of "finishers" would finish their time on earth taking the decades of knowledge and wealth they've amassed and use it to serve humanity, in the name of Jesus.

I also have a vision that hundreds of thousands of young frustrated professionals sitting in cubes would take a chance and create PROFITABLE, productive enterprises that employ people, provide jobs, provide opportunities to use creative skills, and serve humanity.

Do we really need more salty snacks, carbonated beverages, and hamburger restaurants? How about stretching our imagination a bit and thinking about what would serve our city, serve our fellow human? It is possible to create billions in shareholder wealth while legitimately meeting human needs. With this thing called "cloud computing," you essentially have infinite technological capacity out there to start a business service that requires very low startup costs.[41] With 3-D printing, almost anyone can be a product inventor. Combined with thousands of manufacturers in China

---

[40] One book that really challenged me on the need for sustainable development is called Toxic Charity, by Robert Lupton.
[41] Businesses like Uber and AirBnB demonstrate that it really just takes a good idea to create BILLIONS in shareholder value. We often constrain ourselves by capital requirements necessary to scale a business. But in this new "cloud economy," the barriers to entry are remarkably low to bring innovation to the market. Cloud economics allow massive computing power, GPS technology, public databases, and algorithms to maximize the productive use of already existing physical infrastructure. I pray that more and more young Christian professionals will leave their cubicles and start swinging for the fences with new business models.

with spare capacity, you could bring your product to market on platforms like Amazon.com and scale up to meet demand, almost overnight. I could go on and on about the possibilities but what I know is this: If you love the glory of God, if you want to maximize your eternal treasure, if you love your neighbor and want to serve people, you'll figure this out without me. You have permission not to live an ordinary, mediocre life. You have permission to use your creativity to make **LOTS** of money, bless people along the way, and invest that money back for the glory of God.

Work is the engine that creates resources that advance the gospel. Work is the engine that can help you with your own fruitfulness and sanctification. Work is the engine that can help others live productive lives and be a blessing to many. Work is the engine that can lift many out of poverty and mitigate structural sin. Work is an engine that can demonstrate we live in another kingdom, but we are salt and light in the kingdom of this world. And work can be that engine that pays for advancing the gospel to the ends of the earth.

The Extraordinary Work of Prayer

I just described about 2% of the population that has the motivation and drive to create new kingdom enterprises. For the rest of us, we can advance the kingdom in an ordinary, yet extraordinary way. What way is that? PRAYER.

> *The effective, fervent prayer of a righteous man avails much. Elijah was a man with a nature like ours, and he prayed earnestly that it would not rain; and it did not rain on the land for three years and six months. And he prayed again, and the heaven gave rain, and the earth produced its fruit. James 5:16b-18*

I've emphasized work as an engine for kingdom resources because the vast majority of us spend the vast majority of our waking hours at work. But please see that what we are doing with time, talent, and treasure is ultimately spiritual in nature. We are using physical resources to advance a spiritual kingdom. The Holy Spirit through the Church does the decisive work. He uses our ordinary resources like time, talent, and treasure, and he uses extraordinary resources like prayer.

We don't wrestle against flesh and blood. We are engaged in spiritual warfare even as we do mundane tasks like getting our kids ready for school. We are constantly tempted to disqualify ourselves from being fruitful and effective for Christ. *"I don't have a lot of talent and money. I don't own a* business. *I'm not a leader at church. I don't have children to invest in. I don't, I don't..."* Don't let that sin overtake you. All of us can pray and if we actually believe scripture that the power of the Holy Spirit moves in prayer, we would pray more.

Sometimes God wakes me up at very early hours of the morning. In my spirit I know I need to pray and so I intercede for everyone that the Spirit brings to mind: brothers, sisters, friends, unsaved friends, colleagues, pastors, leaders, and so forth. It's like the story of Moses raising his hands over the battlefield. As long as he kept his hands raised, Joshua kept winning the battle in the earthly realm (Exodus 17:11-12). Prayer is the extraordinary means of grace that God gives very ordinary children, women, and men like Elijah to accomplish extraordinary things for his glory.

Grow and invest in your heavenly treasure NOW. What's in your hands? Is it "just" five loaves and two fish? Does that seem insignificant? In God's economy, nothing he gives you is insignificant. PRAY. Little prayer, little power. Much prayer, much power.[42] In God's economy, the greatest work you can do is pray.

A shout-out to mothers

In God's economy, what we do with our time, talent, and treasure that endures for eternity accrues to our heavenly treasure. In this day and age of worldly philosophy, women bear a particular burden. They assume "mental debt" on themselves to be perfect wives, perfect mothers, accomplished career professionals and so on. Speaking directly to mothers, I would like to say a few words of encouragement.

First, the world will tell you that if you go to college but don't have a full and promising career, that you have or are wasting your talent. Nothing could be further from the truth. As you use your gifts and talents in the workplace, you can and should expect to be fully valued and fully compensated for your contribution. The U.S. economy is slowly moving toward recognizing this value. However, both men and women should not look to work to receive validation. In God's economy, we don't validate ourselves by looking at the measuring stick of accomplishment. Our first validation is simply receiving God's acceptance based on justification by faith (Romans 5:1). We simply receive God's approval based on Christ's accomplishment on the cross!

---

[42] This phrase has been attributed to E.M. Bounds and Bishop Julius Calvin Trimble.

Second, pouring yourself into your children and raising them to godly character has ETERNAL CONSEQUENCES (Psalm 112: 2, 3). Our careers will come and go. At some point, we will all learn that our jobs will pass away and once we are gone, our employer will no longer care about us. It's just a fact. But what we invest in the eternal asset column lasts forever. Our kids last forever. So, mothers, your role in raising the children has impact and repercussions that will outlive all the accolades and titles the world could ever give you. You are training up world changers.

Third, living according to God's design will produce the most satisfaction. In other words, when we live our lives according to biblical principles, we receive God's blessings without the sorrow of mental debt (Proverbs 10:22). How many people do you know live their lives for success and end their days full of sorrow and regret? God's ways protect us from the grief and realization that we wasted the best years of our lives in the vain pursuit of personal glory.

So mothers, be encouraged! Whether you stay-at-home, manage a career, or juggle both, you can live God's way for his approval, not the approval of man. The benchmark for success is not measured with titles or pay, but with the satisfaction of knowing that your labors are not in vain in the Lord (1 Corinthians 15:58) as you invest time, talent, and treasure in your children. Your godly legacy, lived out in your children, will last forever and will be rewarded by your heavenly Father.

Chapter 21 – INVEST – In Your Legacy Account
Using Mammon to Grow the Kingdom

And I say to you, make friends for yourselves by unrighteous mammon, that when you fail, they may receive you into an everlasting home. Luke 16:9

In my previous chapter, I wrote about the "GROW – INVEST" paradigm. Grow earthly resource and invest it in what is eternal. What is the purpose of money? The purpose of money is to declare back to God what we think of his glory. If the goal of our lives is to demonstrate the glory of God, then one of the primary vehicles is through money. The problem with money and the reason why the Bible warns against the deceitfulness of riches is that in this life we view money not as a resource, but as the prize, as the scoreboard. In the temporal sense, wealth is an asset. In God's economy earthly wealth is a liability. Once we understand that earthly wealth is a liability, a resource for God's kingdom use, we will free ourselves from the love of money and we will serve our king to advance his kingdom.

Once more, why is earthly wealth a liability? A liability account is like a loan. Loans are seed investment you are entrusted with to produce something of greater value. Our very lives are on loan from God. *"So, teach us to number our days, that we may gain a heart of wisdom"* (Psalm 90:12). We spend our limited time on this earth accumulating resources. We convert time into human capital through education, training, experience, and finally acquiring valuable skill. Skill is recognized by an employer or by customers and we monetize that skill and slowly accumulate earthly wealth. The process of accumulating earthly wealth is LONG and PAINFUL. Because the process of accumulating earthly wealth is LONG and PAINFUL we naturally view wealth as an asset and the PRIZE, not a loan. But in God's economy, the whole point of money is to declare Christ's worth!

> *Worthy is the Lamb who was slain*
> ***To receive** power and **riches** and wisdom,*
> *And blessing and honor and glory and blessing! Revelation 5:12*

Do you see that? The lamb is worthy to receive riches! Why in the world would the Lord, who owns the cattle on a thousand hills want money? The answer is he doesn't want or need money. He is testing our hearts to see whether we value his glory. And so, one way that we demonstrate our love for his glory, is we take that hard earned money, and use it as a resource to advance his kingdom.

In the Parable of the Shrewd Manager (Luke 16:1-15), Jesus notes and praises this dishonest steward of the master's resources. Why is he praiseworthy? Because in the parable, he realizes the jig is up. His time is short and the time of reckoning is at hand. But rather than lament at how he has wasted time and resource, he applies himself and finishes strong. He hustles and collects as much of his master's money as possible.

Jesus then makes the transition from stewarding earthly wealth to growing the kingdom. "Make friends for yourself." What Jesus is referring to is leveraging all of your resources, your money, and your reputation to grow true riches. Your true riches are in your eternal equity account. And to grow true riches, you win souls to Christ. "When it fails," or as another translation says, "When you fail..." This refers to the end of your life. Your life ends and the clock stops ticking. God judges the money you've accumulated. Is the money stuck in your liability account or did you transfer it to your asset account? *"When it fails, they may receive you into eternal dwellings" (Luke 16:9 ESV).*

We should all do the work of an evangelist, but God gives us more resources (especially in America) than we have time to personally spend. I myself have limited means to personally share the gospel. There are only 24 hours in a day and I have a wife and five children and a day job. I am not excused from sharing the gospel; it's just a reality that with my time and my talent, I can only do x-amount. What is exciting is that when I partner with highly effective ministries, missionaries, and pastors and use unrighteous mammon, they can take that money and produce 10x, 100x what I alone could do for the kingdom.

Remember Philippians 4:17? *"Not that I desire the gift, but I desire the fruit that abounds to your account."* The church that was investing in Paul received credit for the amazing amount of fruitfulness Paul produced for the kingdom. If you believe the premise that generosity gets credited to your balance sheet, then it follows to ask, how do I know where to invest? I will give you my own opinions; as difficult as it was to create wealth, it will be similarly difficult to give the wealth away. This will require much wisdom and prayer. Here are some thoughts:[43]

---

[43] I acknowledge that by specifically mentioning ministries in this section that people in other ministries might feel left out. That is of course, not my intent. It's a delicate balancing act to "prime the pump" with specifics and simultaneously acknowledge that there are thousands of worthy ministries and endeavors. Investing wisely will be a challenge and a delight.

1. Local Church. Give to your local church at least the first tithe[44]. Remember, part of your balance sheet includes your own holiness and the church. The Apostle Paul admonishes us to render double honor to those who preach and teach the gospel (1 Timothy 5:17). The context of his message was referring to local elders in the church. The truth of the matter is that your local church may or may not be the best steward for using kingdom resources. Might I suggest that God is testing your patience? God might be testing how anxious and antsy and agitated you get. Many people who give hover over their gift. They don't know how to give and walk away. They are control freaks. Part of our giving is an acknowledgement of God's sovereignty. So, we give to our local church in loving and trusting obedience.

2. Ministries. Find ministries that resonate with you personally. There are literally thousands of non-profits in which to participate with and contribute towards. You are very naturally going to gravitate toward those that resonate with you. Take the time to get to know the leadership. Pray with them. Serve with them. Over time they will show their true colors and you will be able to ascertain their fruitfulness. Personally, I don't like to invest in sinking ships just because I feel sorry for them. I like to invest with ministries that are swinging for the fences and have found a rhythm and cadence that demonstrate fruitfulness.

3. The last and the least. *Whoever is generous to the poor lends to the LORD, and he will repay him for his deed (Proverbs 19:17, ESV).* There's no qualifier in this verse about attaching response card for helping the poor. Personally, I think micro-finance is a fantastic option. Opportunity International provides loans which return at a 98% repayment rate while the working poor work themselves out of poverty. The money grows and recirculates indefinitely, helping more people get out of poverty. What a fantastic return on investment!

4. Adoption. Taking care of widows and orphans is at the heart of being a Christian. (James 1:27) None of us are natural children of God. We are all children of adoption. (Ephesians 1:5) Therefore, taking care of orphans is an acknowledgement of the gospel that until someone intervenes in your life, you and I are like wandering orphans in this world.

---

[44] "Tithe" simply means 10%

5. Individuals. Compassion International and other organizations have fantastic sponsorship programs where you fund the Christian development of a child all the way through high school. Additionally, Compassion selects the top 2% of their children and offer college sponsorship programs. The idea is that if you want to change a nation, you have to build the next generation of leaders. This is long, costly, and well worth it. Systemic corruption will only change when we can seed the top strata of government, business, and the military with future Christian leaders.

6. Teaching Ministries. I support DesiringGod.org and the Church at Brook Hills (David Platt). Other fantastic ministries [among many] include Revive our Hearts and Bible Study Fellowship (BSF). If sound doctrine and the wisdom in applying God's Word are the base foundation for fruitfulness, I praise God for ministries that accurately and faithfully teach the Bible. The Internet gives such ministries a global platform. Indeed, in this day and age of false teachers we should double-down on ministries that teach well.

7. Bible Translation. Wycliffe Bible Translators have been translating the Bible in thousands of languages so that every people group might have a copy of the Bible in their native tongue. In order for every tongue, every tribe, and every nation to bow at the name of Jesus, they need to know who Jesus is. Supporting Bible translation is paramount to completing the Great Commission.

8. Evangelists. Billy Graham, Greg Laurie, Nick Hall, Ravi Zacharias and others are faithfully proclaiming the gospel all over the world. Don't you want some of their fruit credited to your account?

9. Missions. Operation Mobilization, Gospel for Asia, and Cru are taking the gospel to the ends of the earth. They have the expertise, the infrastructure, and the vision to go further and persevere longer. Their track record demonstrates faithfulness to the gospel when so many missions organizations lose their way after decades of institutionalization. Find the missions organizations that keep fidelity to the gospel and resonate with you. Go on a missions trip with them and see what is happening on the front lines.

10. Indigenous pastors and church planters. Through organizations like Gospel for Asia, we directly sponsor church planting pastors. Church planting is the preferred means for advancing the gospel. Think of the local church as an army advancing into hostile territory, carrying and planting the banners of Christ. We are taking ground every day. The

presence of a church validates this. We should not want all the Christians of the world to flee their countries and come to America. Yes, we are a refuge to the world, but we should reverse the equation and go to them, go with them and advance the gospel.

11. If the end goal of all of history culminates with all the nations gathered before the throne of Christ, doesn't it say something about the heart of God and where we should align ourselves? For many, missions and evangelism will NOT resonate personally. There are many reasons why you might prefer digging wells in Africa above gospel proclamation. Both are needed, but remember, only that which endures to eternity is the work of God. Only a small fraction of resources go to the least reached and unreached, the billions who have never heard the gospel. By discipline, my family targets 50% of our allocation toward evangelism and missions.

In God's economy your earthly treasure is *leverage.* In financial terms, leverage means debt. Debt used properly in financing growth compounds returns, when used properly, compounds returns many times over. Leverage works in both directions, however. Debt used improperly can put you under water really quickly. Therefore, as Americans, we need to humbly evaluate all the resources God has given us in time, talent, and treasure. With all the trillions of dollars that evangelicals possess in our stewardship[45], we have the opportunity to finish the Great Commission in our lifetime. Are we up for the task?

---

[45] Don't disqualify yourself if your net worth isn't millions. The average household wealth is a few hundred thousand dollars. That, multiplied across tens of millions of households represents TRILLIONS. Trillions of dollars are an unfathomable, staggering amount of resource that God can use to finish the Great Commission.

Your Legacy Account
Receiving Credit for Others' Fruitfulness

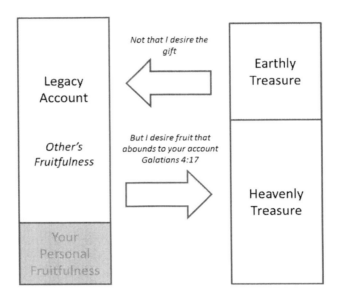

INVEST NOW—What to do with excess wealth

But godliness with contentment is great gain. For we brought nothing into this world, and it is certain we can carry nothing out. 1 Timothy 6:6-7

Generally speaking, as incomes increase, so do standards of living. The nature of money and material possessions is that we are constantly bombarded with advertisements that suggest you are lacking if you do not have certain things. Your life is less fun, less fulfilling, less enjoyable if you do not have, if you can't go, if you don't drive, if you don't possess what the world offers. The world offers an exhausting way to live that produces little to no eternal fruit. But what if we could be freed from this rat race and grow our earthly wealth as a means of growing and advancing the kingdom? Then we would find joy in the capacity God gives us to serve and give, and the gain would be our heavenly treasure.

The first thing about contentment is defining, "How much is enough?" The Bible defines it pretty sparsely – food and clothing (1 Timothy 6:8), not even mentioning a house. Here's the principle behind the scripture. Find a budget, a cash outflow that allows you to be productive and fruitful, living as a citizen of the kingdom and stick to it. If your roof is constantly leaking, fix it. You'll end up spending more kingdom resources by not maintaining your house, by not maintaining your car, by not taking care of your health, by not eating right. Being fruitful in this body requires a good deal of maintenance and a fair amount of cost, especially if you live in the United States.

However, there is a trap that comes with having things. The more you have, the more you have to maintain. This takes your time, talent, and treasure away from godliness and the gospel and you have to focus on stuff. **You need much less than you think.** Just ask the World War II generation how much stuff you actually need to get by. Ask immigrant families who are trying to educate their kids and build a family business how much they actually need to get by. You need far less than you think. Advertisements, T.V., Facebook, your neighbors all suggest that you won't get a thumbs-up if you're not living a glamorous lifestyle. And so, the world conspires to fill you with lust, with covetousness, with insecurity. **The antidote to this is the gospel.**

> *Have this mind among yourselves, which is yours in Christ Jesus, who, though he was in the form of God, did not count equality with God a thing to be grasped, but emptied himself, by taking the form of a servant, being born in the likeness of men. And being found in human form, he humbled himself by becoming obedient to the point of death, even death on a cross. Philippians 2:5-8*

When we understand the gospel and justification, we find our security in Christ alone. We don't need the constant insatiable cravings of the flesh to be fulfilled in order to be secure. We are secure in Christ's perfect sacrifice. When we embrace his example, we can stop thinking about ourselves and we can serve one another in love.

This gospel-motivated attitude changes how we think about money. Over 2/3 of our waking hours are spent on producing wealth or preserving wealth. And the Bible tells us what we should do with all that wealth. We should invest it. NOW

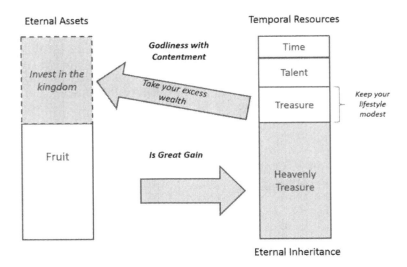

*As for the rich in this present age, charge them not to be haughty, nor to set their hopes on the uncertainty of riches, but on God, who richly provides us with everything to enjoy. They are to **do good, to be rich in good works, to be generous and ready to share, thus storing up treasure for themselves** as a good foundation for the future, so that they may take hold of that which is truly life. 1 Timothy 6:17-19*

Take hold of life! Real life begins after death. This life is a dress rehearsal for the next. This life is SO SHORT. Why would we want to hoard our money now, when we could invest it in advancing the kingdom and thus secure our heavenly treasure?

Look at the phrase, "storing up treasures for themselves." We set our hope on God. We set our hope on things that are eternal and we pour ourselves into that which endures. Our treasure is Christ himself and he will give us increased capacity in the next life to glorify him through increased responsibilities. Godliness with contentment is *mega-porismos [Greek]*, great gain. That gain is profit in our eternal equity.

There are so many questions that arise from this concept of living a lifestyle that is moderate and investing the rest in the kingdom: How much should I live on? How much should I leave my children as an inheritance? Where should I give the money to? How do I know the money will be put to good use? These are legitimate questions, but don't let the questions rob you of your joy.[46] Don't let the unresolved questions take away from the one needful question: Is Christ worthy? Does he deserve everything? If you can resonate with the vision of the exaltation of Christ, that at the name of Jesus every knee will bow, then you will find your purpose in this life. And that purpose is to use your time, talent, and treasure, all of it, to glorify his name.

Believe it or not, there's math behind the "*mega-porismos*," the great-gain. Essentially, giving a $1,000 charitable gift now is worth multiples of giving $1,000 when you die. There are several reasons why this is true:

1) Your gift escapes estate taxes

2) Your gift accrues investment returns tax-free in your charity

3) Your gifts are deductible from your annual income taxes

Charitable Gift Example

So, here's the math:

Multiplicative Value of the Gift = <u>Future Value of the Gift</u>
                                        <u>Future Value in your will</u>

(source: CFA Institute)

Say you're 40 years old, you have a spouse and two kids, and you're wondering, "Should I give $1,000 to charity now? Shouldn't I invest that $1,000 in the market, generate a return, and then it will be worth more as a bequest when I die? That's how most people think. The mathematical answer is NO! If you give that $1,000 now the multiplicative value is the following:

$$(1+7\%)^{30} + 35\%*[1 +(7\%*(1-35\%))]^{30}* (1 – 50\%)$$
Divided by
$$[1 +(7\%*(1-35\%))]^{30}* (1 – 50\%)$$

---

[46] I recommend any book by Randy Alcorn to go more in detail on money and lifestyle issues, like <u>Money, Possessions and Eternity</u>.

That equates to a **436% increase** in the value of your gift if you give it now vs. waiting till you're 70 and die.[47] Even if you're 60 years old and you're thinking, "I want to enjoy my final years and I can hold off on giving another 10 years," the math equates to over a **200% increase** in the value of the gift. The time value of money and the tax-shields provided by charitable giving provide a great incentive to GIVE NOW.[48]

The other reason why giving now is important, beyond the dollar return on your investment is that you need to build habits of godliness. Generosity is a muscle. Almost nobody is naturally generous when it comes to money. The reason why is your tendency is to think *about other things you'd rather be doing* with the money than giving. We need to train our brains, our hearts, and our wallets to respond daily to the gospel. When we think about the amazing sacrifice of Jesus Christ, we bring the sacrifice of praise, we bring our first fruits of giving, and we offer ourselves as living sacrifices to God. That is the acceptable response of worship to a God who graciously gave us everything through the life, death, and resurrection of his son, Jesus Christ.

Put it this way, if you don't start giving now, chances are you won't be generous at the end of your life. Your habits tend to accumulate and become very hard to break. There is only one needful question when it comes to money: Is Christ worthy? We all know the answer to that.

---

[47] I'm assuming just for math that the donor lives to the age of 70.
[48] Obviously everyone's tax rates and returns on capital will be different, but the math properly illustrates the power of compounding interest, time, and tax-shields to the benefit of giving.

Chapter 22 – FINISH STRONG – Confidence
Invest in Steve Jobs or Jesus?

"Assuredly, I say to you, there is no one who has left house or brothers or sisters or father or mother or wife or children or lands, for My sake and the gospel's, who shall not receive a hundredfold now in this time—houses and brothers and sisters and mothers and children and lands, with persecutions— and in the age to come, eternal life. But many who are first will be last, and the last first. Mark 10:29 – 31

If you invested in Apple stock when Steve Jobs returned to the helm in 1997, you would have purchased the stock at around $7 per share. The stock peaked in September 2012 at $700. Such an investor would have realized over a 100x return on investment. In this scenario, you were essentially investing in your faith in Steve Jobs. Faith in the management team plays a large role in long term investments. In the same way, trusting Christ with everything demonstrates what we believe he will do with our investment.

When an investor evaluates a company to invest in, he scrutinizes the quality of the CEO. Where has this CEO worked before? What roles has he played? What kind of results has he delivered? How credible is he in making and keeping promises? Obviously the higher the credibility, the more investors will take risk investing in the vision of such a CEO. In fact, when Steve Jobs was alive, if you backed out the intrinsic value of the company the stock price had a 20% premium on top. This meant investors were anticipating that Steve would deliver on promises he hadn't even made yet. To use biblical language, Steve would give more than they could ask or imagine.

When Steve was alive, people were throwing their money at Apple stock. And yet when it comes to investing with King Jesus, Christians (including me) are constantly hedging their bets.

Jesus promises a hundred-fold return on our investment in the kingdom. He illustrates the return using words like "houses, land, brothers, and sisters." What does he mean? What he means is that as his Church grows we will be able to see his kingdom expand with more men and women who are our spiritual "brothers and sisters." I have shared a warm meal with Christians in "houses and lands" all over the world. The genuine hospitality reflected the unity of the Holy Spirit that exists with believers everywhere. It's not hidden and esoteric. I remember going to a Promise Keepers rally with 50,000 men. My friends and I kept saying, "This is so cool. Wow, I can't believe there are so many of us."

Jesus used the word picture of a mustard seed to illustrate how the kingdom starts off as a small speck and then grows into a mighty tree. And, if you look at the history of the Church you will see that Christianity explodes in growth after long periods of persecution. Some organizations estimate that there are over 100 million Christians in China! Jesus said he would build his church and the gates of hell would not prevail against us.

So, the kingdom continues to advance after 2,000 years. Jesus, our Chief Executive, has proven himself true to his commitments. Shouldn't we double down? Why is there so much pessimism among American Christians when it comes to investing in the kingdom? *Where your treasure is, there your heart will be also (Matthew 6:21).*

Pessimism creates a downward spiral, a vicious cycle. We saw this in the 2008 economic crisis. When people see no hope for the future, they pull their money out of investments. When people pull their money out of investments, you see an implosion in the stock market. Many analysts and historians note how close the entire global economy came to completely imploding. Money is meant to be circulated.

Similarly, many Christians have no expectation of a return when they donate money. To many it's like throwing good money away. They view giving as "charity" and not as investing. So, when they give, they literally are not thinking about any return. Hence, they invest as little as possible.

Many people simply doubt Christ's promises. Unlike the bullish faith millions of people placed in Steve Jobs to lead Apple, many Christians exhibit a lack of confidence in Jesus Christ. Sure God has proven himself over and over in our lives but how often do we forget the answered prayers of last year? Our spiritual memories quickly tend toward amnesia. We forget God's faithfulness and worry incessantly about the future. Rather than trusting Christ and investing in him, we trust in ourselves and hence we place all of our time, talent, and treasure in self-focused schemes, goals, and plans.

We may be tempted to gloss over Jesus' lavish promise of a hundredfold return. How can I cash in on the fact that the kingdom advances one hundred times over (Mark 10:45)? I can't eat that. I can't go on vacation with that. I can't buy new clothes with that. I can't buy a car with that. We value material possessions and hence store up our treasure on this earth, where moth and rust corrupt. We think it's so great to buy new gadgets but feeding starving families on the other side of the world? I'll do just enough not to feel guilty. I undervalue what that money is doing. I don't allow myself to receive joy when I penny pinch my giving.

When we think about heavenly treasure, we imagine white puffy clouds and halos. Who cares? I'd rather spend my hard earned money on going to white sandy beaches in Cancun. No, if I really saw with spiritual eyes the value of Christ's name, and Christ's reputation advancing to the ends of the earth, I would value that. I would prize that. I would deem that worthy.

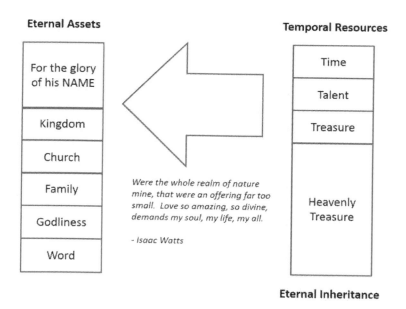

Stop giving out of guilt. Go all out for the kingdom so that Christ's name and his glory might cover the earth like the waters cover the sea.

Investing in earthly equity requires scrutinizing the credibility of the CEO that you are investing in. You are examining follow through on past promises, future potential growth, and your confidence that he can keep his promises. We would have no problem investing in Steve Jobs. Investing in the kingdom is like placing a vote of confidence in King Jesus. Believe in his promises, go all in, and you will receive a 100x return.

Chapter 23 – FINISH STRONG – Wealth Transfer

How to Transfer Wealth for the Glory of God

If then you have not been faithful in the unrighteous wealth, who will entrust to you the true riches? Luke 16:11

I've written about the "Grow—Invest" paradigm from the standpoint of younger, maturing Christians who still hypothetically have decades left in their lives. In "Grow—Invest" you simultaneously grow your resource base while investing in eternal fruit. But there's a segment of Christians who are looking backwards with some regret. They are looking at the "success to significance" paradigm as a comforting thought. Let me speak specifically to the retiring generation about how to transfer the wealth you've accrued for the glory of God.

When you die, you will have no more time, your human capital (talent) will be spent, and what's left on your eternal balance sheet is this massive liability called earthly treasure. God will call your loan. Now you're trying to determine what to do with all that treasure before he calls you home. If you're in the process of reviewing and updating your will, I have a few suggestions to orient you towards finishing strong for the glory of God.

Family
An inheritance gained hastily at the beginning will not be blessed at the end. Proverbs 20:21

Give to your children and grandchildren **just enough to help them be fruitful**. An example might mean paying for college and a down payment on a house. Beyond that, I would really pray hard and seek godly counsel. While I cannot address every personal situation, what I do know is this: Too much money spoils fruitfulness, both the fruit of growing earthly resources and eternal assets. In order to generate earthly wealth, you need commitment. "Commit your way to the Lord and he will establish your paths." In Hebrew, the word "commit" is *"galal."* *Galal* literally means rolling a large rock. In the business world, we have a similar image of moving a flywheel. A flywheel is a heavy object that once it gets moving continues to generate momentum to power an engine. How much effort is required to move a flywheel? I go back to my 10,000 hours rule. It takes sheer persistence and sweat to do well in college, start a career, excel in a career, earn a reputation for excellence, and then reap the benefits of that reputation. With too much unearned money to fall back on, I've seen plenty of people give up when they encounter difficulty. They never push that flywheel. Furthermore, having unearned wealth creates a tendency to rely on wealth and not on Christ for strength (Proverbs 10:15). While not written in stone, that tendency is strong. The amount you should bequeath to your children's children is between you and the Lord. I believe if you give too much money and spoil your descendants' fruitfulness this will be held against your eternal equity. Seek godly counsel. I'd recommend calling the National Christian Foundation as a starting point. (www.nationalchristian.com)

Church

Honor the Lord with your wealth and with the firstfruits of all your produce; then your barns will be filled with plenty, and your vats will be bursting with wine. Proverbs 3:9-10

Giving to the local church is a sticking point for many people, a sore spot. Why? Because many of us spend so much of our time assessing, evaluating, scrutinizing, judging our pastors and we use money as our weapon. We cling to our checkbooks and rationalize our lack of giving to our local church as "stewardship." "Well, if they were more responsible, I'd give more." Don't be deceived. That is only partly true. If building eternal assets is the goal of your life, then godliness will be a top priority. And with godliness comes generosity. We should be generous to our church and to our pastors. It's that simple.

> *"For it is written in the Law of Moses, "You shall not muzzle an ox when it treads out the grain." Is it for oxen that God is concerned? Does he not certainly speak for our sake? It was written for our sake, because the plowman should plow in hope and the thresher thresh in hope of sharing in the crop. If we have sown spiritual things among you, is it too much if we reap material things from you? 1 Corinthians 9:9-11*

I just don't understand why many people believe that those who follow the path of full-time professional ministry should live in substandard housing, drive substandard cars, and live a lifestyle that we would not dare to live ourselves. We think for them that this is the path of godliness because they are following God's call? **But for ourselves we want the best that money can buy?** What kind of hypocrisy goes into that thinking? For professional ministers they should take a vow of poverty but for the rest of us, we deserve nice things? I don't get it. This comes from that very sick thinking that there is a division between sacred and secular and this is not so. "Let the elders who rule well be considered worthy of double honor, especially those who labor in preaching and teaching" (1Timothy 5:17).

We should be generous toward our local church. I am writing about our personal fruit, our personal godliness and spiritual maturity, not about the church's stewardship.[49] **God will judge your church's elders on how the money is spent.** Obviously, if your church lacks controls against fraud, waste, and abuse, step up and do something. You and I know that 99% of the time, that is not the case and giving to your local church is a heart issue. Personally, I use the 10% tithe as a starting point for giving to the local church.

Kingdom and Kingdom Legacy
Seek first the kingdom of God and his righteousness... Matthew 6:33a

God has blessed many of us with excess wealth, and I mean **excess**. If our purpose in life is to grow eternal assets to the glory of God, then having excess wealth forces us toward bigger visions, larger projects, kingdom level endeavors. To the extent that your local church can be a conduit for kingdom projects that are visionary and force you to stretch your faith, may I encourage you to channel funds through that venue? However, I do know that most local churches simply don't have the capacity or infrastructure to stretch as far as you would like to go. This is where the fun begins. You invested practically your whole life to attain the wealth. You will spend the rest of your life to give it away well. And I do mean "well." Well means doing the right due diligence so that the endeavors are fruitful. That means taking the time to kick the tires, go on vision trips, serve where appropriate, and pray with leaders of kingdom initiatives. Blood, sweat, and tears are part of the equation. No half-stepping this.

What is a kingdom initiative? A kingdom initiative is a project, a program, a business, a ministry, or other vehicle that creates the conditions for success so that the Church might flourish around the world. When I say Church, I mean the people, not the buildings or the denominations, per se. In this, let your imagination and creativity go wild! Think of kingdom initiatives as the intersection between huge need, huge faith, and huge opportunity for Christ to be exalted. Invest in the kingdom. This is difficult, but if you have

---

[49] Church stewardship by the Board of Elders is a separate topic. It is certainly worthy of scrutiny and discussion...another book...another day.

generated lots of earthly wealth, that wealth forces you "up the stack" on the eternal balance sheet to be a kingdom person.

Other Philanthropy?

Now, I know what some people are thinking, "Can I give to my local symphony orchestra, the local hospital, my alma mater, etc.?" What is kingdom and what is not kingdom giving? *"Who are you to pass judgment on the servant of another? It is before his own master that he stands or falls. And he will be upheld, for the Lord is able to make him stand" (Romans 14:4).*

Listen, don't let me stand in the way of you giving generously to your college or to a hospital. Who am I to judge the heart? But let me at least give a few observations: One, the more earthly wealth you have, the less likely you are to give to causes that involve evangelism. Part of the reason is that the wealthier you become, the more you socialize with other wealthy people, many of whom are not Christians. They will invite you to this fund-raiser, that cocktail party, this wine and cheese party, and that endeavor. In those circles, drilling wells in Africa may be in vogue, talking about Jesus is usually not.

Personally, I am very enthusiastic about giving to causes that improve human flourishing. Some people view anything that is not "proclamation" as "social gospel." Not so. In my previous chapter on the kingdom, I wrote about creating conditions so that the Church can be fruitful. This involves much MORE than proclamation. This requires sustainable partnership. With TRILLIONS of dollars of wealth, American Evangelicals can invest in sustainability and complete the Great Commission. We have more than enough resources to do both.

Sustainable development always includes a vibrant passion for the person of Christ above the specific cause. There's only one king, JESUS. If his name is not highly exalted in all of our "compassionate" endeavors, we are building on sinking sand. The sophisticated elites will not want to hear his name at their cocktail parties and fundraisers. But his name is exalted and we should long for his name to cover the earth like the waters cover the sea.

We extend his name through our time, talent, and treasure. By the end of your life, your time will be gone, your human capital spent, and all that will be left on your liability column will be earthly wealth. Should God bless you with long life and earthly prosperity, you will naturally start to plan intergenerational wealth transfer. While not addressing every personal circumstance regarding wealth transfer, what should be more than obvious by now is this: What you do with earthly wealth ultimately speaks volumes of what you think of God's glory versus your glory. Do any of us dare to hoard the wealth when he has so graciously given us all things in Christ?

Wealth Transfer

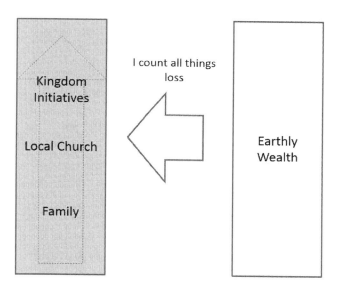

A Word to Gen X-ers and Millenials

Most likely, the tens of trillions of dollars I've been referencing in this book will not be allocated to kingdom purposes. Gen-Xers and Millenials will receive a huge portion of this wealth. Because the average amount of wealth that will be bequeathed will be hundreds of thousands of dollars per recipient and not millions, it would be tempting to view the money as a means of buying a big house or spending on other pleasures.

That is my nightmare scenario.

Tens of trillions of dollars will pass hands over the next 20 years and almost no one is talking about this once in 2,000 year opportunity to apply that resource toward kingdom purposes. My nightmare is that young millennials will receive the bequeathed money and say, "Thanks Mom, Dad,

Grandma, Grandpa," lever up, and buy a massive house. Leverage on top of tens of trillions of dollars in real estate will create the largest bubble in the history of the planet. Such a scenario can't end well.

Gen-Xers. Millenials. I pray that we seize the opportunity of this massive wealth transfer in our lifetimes and go all out for the gospel. We can do it. We can complete the Great Commission. All the chips are on the table. We get one shot at life. Will we make it count for eternity?

Further Resources:

If you have not done so, I would recommend contacting the National Christian Foundation (www.nationalchristian.com) about setting up a donor-advised fund (DAF). A DAF is a tax-sheltered vehicle for generosity. They would be thrilled to walk you through the generosity journey.

Chapter 24 – FINISH STRONG – Death
Securing your Gains

For to me, to live is Christ, and to die is gain. Philippians 1:21

If we believed certain truths about God's economy, our lives would undergo a radical transformation. We would live every day as if we were on borrowed time, living for the glory of God to the maximum, and pressing in to advance God's kingdom. This would grow our eternal asset account. There is a profit that is waiting for us but, for now is only "paper" profit. When we die and are with the Lord, all those "paper" profits are converted into gain.

In the book of Philippians, we see Paul's heart. He wants so much for his fellow Christian to live out the fruit of righteousness.

> *And this I pray, that your love may abound still more and more in knowledge and all discernment, that you may approve the things that are excellent, that you may be sincere and without offense till the day of Christ, **being filled with the fruits of righteousness** which are by Jesus Christ, to the glory and praise of God. Philippians 1:6-11*

When you live for the glory of God, when you produce the fruits of righteousness, your eternal asset accounts grow. When you care about heavenly treasure you press in to advance the kingdom, even if it means chains, even if it means suffering, because Christ is worthy.

And Paul has this dilemma: He is close to finishing his race. He has not only started many churches, but has discipled and trained them to be fruit bearing. His account is overflowing and he can say with confidence that he has lived for the sake of Christ. Paul is ready to secure his gains. What stands in his way? Two things: love, and death.

> *For to me, **to live is Christ, and to die is gain**. But if I live on in the flesh, this will mean fruit from my labor; yet what I shall choose I cannot tell. For I am hard-pressed between the two, having a desire to depart and be with Christ, which is far better. Nevertheless to remain in the flesh is more needful for you. Philippians 1:21-24*

"To live is Christ." Paul loves his congregation in Philippi. He wants to produce more fruit in them through his hard work. He believes they still need him. But oh, he wants to be with Christ! *"In your presence is fullness of joy. At your right hand are pleasures forevermore" (Psalm 16:11)*

Do you want to be with Christ? Do you desire his presence? Do you want to see his glory? I can say with sadness that all too often the trappings of this world blind and deceive me and I think about all I would be leaving behind. I'm worse than Lot's wife.

"To die is gain." Satan does not want you to believe this truth. What Satan whispers in your ears is, "To die is LOSS." Think of all you would lose? You start imagining graduations, weddings, and vacations with your kids and grandkids, all the life events you want to see. And what happens, is you build up these events in your mind to be more worthy than Christ. And so the thought of dying and being with the Lord fills you with dread, not happiness.

When the thought of dying and being with the Lord fills you with sorrow, how you live today will reflect that. You won't go all out for the kingdom. You won't live in such a way as to advance the gospel (Hebrews 2:14-15). You won't produce the fruits of righteousness. Maybe for you, to live is not Christ. To live is to live for the American Dream.

What a tragedy! What an absolute travesty! We're trying to make everything in church relevant, so that Christianity fits nicely and neatly into living in a nice house, having a nice yard, driving a nice car, working at a nice job, petting a nice dog. The thought of sacrificing any of that for the sake of the gospel is sheer madness! And to leave that behind and be with Christ? No way! I'm sticking around as long as I can.

"To die is gain." This word "gain" in Greek is *"kerdos,"* which means "profit, gain." If you were to buy a fixer-upper house for say, $100k and sell it for $250k, you would book a profit (*porismos*). Many people do this. They pour themselves in to remodeling the kitchen, remodeling the bathrooms, improving curb appeal, all to book a gain. The thought of increasing the value of their home motivates many people! They work tireless hours to book that gain. Now the truth of the matter is that the market value of your house might be an incremental +$150k profit. But that is only paper profit. You don't actually have a profit (*kerdos*) until you make a transaction that secures your gain.

And so it is with life. We can work all our lives for the Lord producing fruit. What secures our profit is finishing the race. Believe it or not, there are Christians who tragically start strong and finish poorly. Their fruit rots and goes bad because of vain glory. They started out doing things for the glory of God, but by the end of their lives their work was to puff themselves up. Bad fruit. No, what secures your gain *(kerdos)* is finishing strong and then crossing the river to be with the Lord. When you live for the glory of God and you are confident in the race you have run, you can say, "Being with Christ is far better."

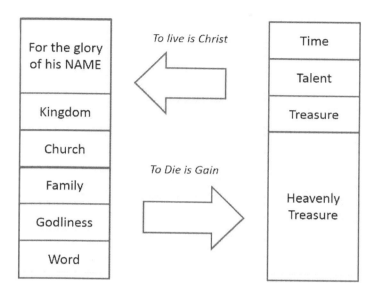

Live to Die, Die to Live
Unless a grain of wheat falls into the ground and dies, it remains alone. John 12:24

Our life in God's economy is one big paradox. Save your life, you lose it. Lose your life for Christ, you find it (Luke 17:33). The reason why is because the way of the cross is death. Death to self is like fertilizer for a bumper crop. We are put on this earth to die to ourselves, our dreams, and our bucket lists so that Christ might be exalted. And instead of thinking of death as a waste, death to self is the seed that produces fruit, eternal fruit. That eternal fruit is gain. That gain abounds to our inheritance. Our inheritance is God's recognition, reward, and responsibility. This life is practice for the life to come. **Our inheritance is waiting for us.**

> *Most assuredly, I say to you, unless a grain of wheat falls into the ground and dies, it remains alone; but if it dies, it produces much*

grain. He who loves his life will lose it, and he who hates his life in this world will keep it for eternal life. John 12:24-25

When we cross the Jordan River, perhaps we will hear the Hallelujah chorus, and as we run into arms of our savior, we will hear,

> The kingdom of this world is become, the kingdom of our Lord and of his Christ, and of his Christ...and of his Christ...and he shall reign forever and ever...King of Kings....and Lord of Lords...and he shall reign forever and ever...[50]

The Song in My Head

> When I survey the wondrous cross
> On which the Prince of glory died,
> My richest gain I count but loss,
> And pour contempt on all my pride.
>
> Forbid it, Lord, that I should boast,
> Save in the death of Christ my God!
> All the vain things that charm me most,
> I sacrifice them to His blood.
>
> See from His head, His hands, His feet,
> Sorrow and love flow mingled down!
> Did e'er such love and sorrow meet,
> Or thorns compose so rich a crown?
>
> **Were the whole realm of nature mine,**
> **That were a present far too small;**
> **Love so amazing, so divine,**
> **Demands my soul, my life, my all.**

-      Isaac Watts, Hymns and Spiritual Songs (1707)

---

[50] From Handel's *Messiah*

Made in the USA
Lexington, KY
27 March 2015